"If you've ever felt unknown in a crowded room or close to God but far from people, you're not alone. This book speaks to that ache and offers a biblical path toward the kind of connection your soul was made for."

BEN BENNETT, Speaker; Author; Cofounder, Resolution Movement

"Shelby doesn't write from a distance. He writes from the middle of the mess—naming the real, raw struggles that so many young people face, without sugarcoating or condescending. This book goes after the actual roots of loneliness with both truth and tenderness, pairing a deep grasp of the gospel with practical, soul-level help. Shelby has a rare gift for speaking with his readers, not at them, and that authenticity makes all the difference. Every chapter feels like a conversation with someone who has been there, who isn't afraid to say the hard thing, and who wholeheartedly believes that Jesus has the power to meet us in our loneliest places and bring lasting change."

AMY LYNCH, Author, *The Nehemiah Way: Mobilizing a Church Full of Leaders*; Founder and CEO, Fernling Press

"Shelby's book on loneliness is a rare combination of power and purity. Power, as there were moments that I found myself shouting at the insightful diagnoses of our current cultural climate. Pure, because, like medicine, truth seeped into my own heart, especially as it relates to empathy toward others. If you're struggling with loneliness as a student or young adult, or quite frankly at any other stage of life, you will be brought to your knees in prayer. A timely, timely book for this generation!"

RECHAB GRAY, Pastor of Preaching and Spiritual Transformation, New Creation Fellowship, Orlando, FL

"God said, 'It is not good for man to be alone,' and I think we'd agree. We were created for meaningful connection with others but too often can't escape the haunting feeling of being alone. With wise and winsome candor, *Why We're Feeling Lonely* helps diagnose what contributes to our loneliness and points us to meaningful ways to develop deep, life-giving relationships as God intends for us to have. I commend it!"

GARRETT KELL, Pastor, Del Ray Baptist Church; Author, *Pure in Heart: Sexual Sin and the Promises of God*

"Shelby Abbott's excellent book helps readers grapple with the questions we should all ask regarding the loneliness epidemic that continues to surge—especially among the younger generations. He invites readers to explore the poisonous substitutes that work as counterfeit sources of belonging. I loved reading this book and thinking more deeply about what Abbott calls "gospel friendships," and how to bond more deeply with others in overlooked and deeply biblical ways. Don't miss this book!"

HEATHER HOLLEMAN, PhD, Speaker; Author, *The Six Conversations: Pathways to Connecting in an Age of Isolation and Incivility*

"Campus ministers, youth-group leaders, or anyone discipling a young person struggling with loneliness—this is the resource you're looking for. With empathy and clarity, Shelby identifies the root causes of Gen Z's isolation and then combats them with biblical truth, practical tips, and thought-provoking questions. Easy to read, timely, and gospel-centered, this book is perfect for one-on-one or small-group discussions with the 'Loneliest Generation'."

SARAH EEKHOFF ZYLSTRA, Senior Writer, The Gospel Coalition

"Every single person feels lonely at times, and sometimes we just don't know how to navigate it. I love this book because it's relevant, real, practical, and biblical. It's going to help every person that reads it!"

ANN WILSON, Host, FamilyLife Today podcast

"Through easy-to-read, illustration-filled chapters, Shelby helps us see that real, unfiltered, other-person-centred commitment to the messy yet beautiful gift of the local church, centred around Jesus, is God's wonderful answer to the epidemic of loneliness. It helped me realise again the joy and privilege of being friends with a God who woos and pursues me, and the possibility of unexpected friendships within the church. As a local church pastor on a council estate full of lonely and isolated people, it's a joy for me to see a wonderful and realistic picture of how our little body of believers, even in its messiness, can bring hope to those who are hopelessly lonely, socially isolated, and totally detached."

SAM GIBB, Pastor, Hope Church Vauxhall, London, UK

"This book convicted, encouraged, and deeply healed me in my struggle with loneliness. Even while surrounded by an amazing community, I often felt unseen—but Shelby Abbott gently exposed how self-centeredness can sometimes hide beneath that kind of loneliness. His words drew me to meditate on Scripture, sit in God's presence, and pursue deeper, selfless connection with others. God's design for meaningful relationships—with him and with people—is beautifully unpacked here. I'm walking away with renewed purpose and perspective, and I'm incredibly grateful for how this book has changed my life."

SIERRA WILSON, Gen-Z reader

Why We're Feeling Lonely (and What We Can Do About It)

Published by:
The Good Book Company

thegoodbook.com | thegoodbook.co.uk
thegoodbook.com.au | thegoodbook.co.nz

Every book published by The Good Book Company has been written by a human author and edited by a human editor. While AI tools are sometimes used to assist with research and support certain processes, all content has been created by a human author and thoroughly checked by our editorial team to ensure it is biblically faithful and pastorally wise.

Cover design by Studio Gearbox | Design and art direction by André Parker

ISBN: 9781802543681 | JOB-008320 | Printed in India

why we're feeling lonely

Shelby Abbott

To Gabe Mahalik and Brian Barnett (my Jonathans).
True friends who have been there for me in the ups and downs of life.
Guys, I love Jesus more because of you.

Contents

Foreword

PAUL DAVID TRIPP

He hung there in incredible physical pain and anguish, naked and nailed to a cross that had been jammed into the ground. The nails ripped at the flesh of his hands and feet. Crucifixion was one of the most tortuous forms of execution the human community has ever known. You wouldn't die right away. No, hours would go by as you hung in unspeakable pain while the mocking crowd gawked at you. But the most horrible thing for Jesus, as he hung there between heaven and earth, numbered with common criminals, wasn't physical pain—it was something relational. His greatest point of distress was the moment when he cried out, "Eli, Eli, lema sabachthani?"—that is, "My God, my God, why have you forsaken me?" (Matthew 27:46).

Jesus had lived, in the endless forever of eternity, in a relationship of perfect love and unity with God the Father. It is the kind of relationship that all of our hearts long for, but that we will not fully experience until all those who have placed their trust in Jesus are with him in the eternity that is to come. There was never a moment of anger between Jesus and the Father, never a moment of disagreement, and never even the slightest moment of separation. There was only perfect love and perfect unity. But on the cross, something shocking happened. The Father turned his back on the Son. Jesus, bearing our sin, experienced what sin does to all of us—it separates us from God. So, in his deepest moment of anguish, he cried out, "My God, my God, why have you forsaken me?"

This question of Jesus was anguish crying out for love. And there is something that you may have missed in this dramatic moment of suffering. In anguish, Jesus prayed to his Father, and what he got in return was complete silence. It was one of those moments in human history when the silence was truly deadening. We all hate rejection. From the little moments of rejection on the playground to the horrible experience of a loved one turning their back on us and walking away, we find rejection deeply painful. But none of us has experienced relational pain at the depth that Jesus experienced on the cross.

Why? Why was it necessary for Jesus to endure this unthinkable separation from God the Father? The answer is found in understanding that Jesus was on the cross as our substitute, not only in his death—paying the price for human sin, which is death (Romans 6:23)—but also in his exclusion from fellowship with his Father, because sin separates us from God (Isaiah 59:2). He was willing to endure his Father's rejection so that we would never again see the back of God's head. Because of his exclusion, we can be reconciled to God, never again living in fear of his rejection.

What does this moment on the cross have to do with our loneliness? The brief answer is: everything! In the perfection of the Garden of Eden, Adam and Eve lived in perfect harmony and love. There was no conflict, no perversion, no rejection, no betrayal, and there were no feelings of alienation, separation, or loneliness. But when Adam and Eve became alienated from God, separate from him because of their disobedience, they immediately became alienated from one another. All human separation, alienation, and loneliness can be traced back to this horrible moment when, for the first time, Adam and Eve were hiding in fear from God and separate from one another.

From that moment on, human beings have had to endure not only separation from God but from one another. And because this is true, millions of us are sadly lonely. Jesus came, once and for all, to flip the script. In his life, death, resurrection, and ascension, he not only unites us to God but invites us into loving community with one another. The good news of the gospel isn't just the restoration of relationship with God but also relationship with our neighbor.

So, because of everything that I have just written, I am very thankful for the book you are about to read. Shelby Abbott knows his Lord, he knows his Bible, he understands the gospel of Jesus Christ, and he knows the real-life struggles of his readers. These things combine to give you a book that is loaded with honest and compassionate wisdom that is easy to understand and apply to your life. Here is a book written by a man who knows what he's talking about, not just because he has walked in your shoes but, more importantly, because he understands the will and the ways of the Savior, who is the ultimate friend of the lonely.

So, settle in and read slowly. Take notes along the way. Read with a couple of friends and discuss what you have read. Turn off your phone to consider and answer the questions at the end of every chapter. If you identify struggles or addictions along the way that you can't solve on your own, seek the help and wisdom of a mature and godly person near you. And approach all of these things with an open and humble heart. You will be glad you did.

Paul David Tripp
President, Paul Tripp Ministries

INTRODUCTION

The Loneliness Epidemic

"I feel so lonely, I could die."

Elvis Presley

"I don't feel called to you anymore." That's what Christians say when they want to break up with you but don't really want to use the phrase "I don't like you anymore."

After several months of dating, my girlfriend had uttered those words and consequently brought me up to speed on her new calling from the Lord... which didn't include me. It was over. I'd thought that she was the one I was going to marry, but I guess I thought wrong. Afterward, as I sat alone on the couch eating cereal at 11 p.m. while watching professional wrestling, there was a dull pain in my belly that felt different from the average stomachache. It lingered and wouldn't go away. It pulsated and kept reminding me of the fact that I was no longer in a romantic relationship with the girl I liked so much.

Sure, the one-bedroom apartment highlighted my aloneness, but this was worse than just being on my own. No, this pain wasn't because I was physically by myself; it wasn't even the pain of rejection. The pain was present because I was lonely, and frankly, loneliness sucks.

A Unique Life Stage

Natalie is a senior at George Mason University right outside of Washington, D.C. She confided that she felt incredibly lonely despite being constantly surrounded by her peers on campus in the dorm, in the dining hall, in class, and even casually hanging around in the student center. She doesn't seem to connect with anyone around her, and as a result, she has had major battles with mental health and depression since going off to college. It's weighed her down, impacted her grades, and even altered her appetite.

Josh is a sophomore at Virginia Tech. As we met one afternoon to talk and hang out, he told me that his battle with loneliness over the last two years at school has rekindled temptations to harm himself and even struggles with suicidal thoughts. He showed me a few scars he had from cutting his arms back when he was in high school, and I felt overwhelmed with sadness and compassion for him. I'm glad to say he's more deeply involved in a campus ministry now, and that's helping, but he still wrestles with the kind of dark desires that come from feeling isolated.

Sam graduated from high school a year ago and works at a construction company in eastern Pennsylvania. He's still dating the girl he was with last year as a senior, but admitted to me one evening that life just isn't the same as it was when he was in school. He's with other people all the time on construction sites and even spends plenty of time with his girlfriend, but loneliness still creeps up on him almost every day. He told me how much he misses the social life he used to have in high school, and his longing for the way it used to be makes his loneliness even more profound.

Malika turns 30 in two months and just moved out of her dad's house to get an apartment on her own in Orlando, Florida. She's single and loves spending time with friends, but she confessed to me and a few other people on a video call one day that moving out on her own has generated a significant amount of anxiousness, fear, and loneliness in her life. She loves having her own place and independence, but there's also a big part of her that hates it at the same time. Sometimes at night before she goes to bed, she feels scared and isolated to the point that it impacts her ability to sleep and feel rested.

I've been working with college students for over two decades now, and in my ministry with them, I've had a front-row seat to the struggles young people like you experience and wrestle with. When we begin to face life's hardships as a new adult, perhaps with more independence than we've experienced before, there's a particular kind of loneliness that can take its toll.

The four examples I just gave are anecdotal, but Natalie, Josh, Sam, and Malika are real people—and their problem with feeling lonely isn't uncommon. The struggle is everywhere today. In fact, nearly all the significant ministry conversations I've had with 20-somethings in the last year or so have had the common denominator of a fight with loneliness.

A Public Health Concern

Nobody wants to be lonely. I've never met a person who would say that they love to be by themselves all the time, detached from everyone and everything.

You might be an introverted person who says you'd prefer to spend your weekends alone, tucked away from the world. But I'd be willing to bet that if I pried a little to find out what you did, you may well have spent your "me time" in some kind of connection with others in the form of social media or playing interactive video games. So though you might be alone on Friday through Sunday each week, many of your choices probably involve interacting with other people—albeit digitally. In a sense, we often elect to spend our "alone time" with other human beings. But why? Why do we choose—even when we're alone—to connect with other people?

Because loneliness, for anyone and everyone, is hellish.

A recent U.S. poll found that one in every four young adults feels lonely "a lot of the day."[1] I'm not sure how much daily time "a lot" is, but in another survey, 73% of 18-22-year-olds reported "sometimes or always feeling alone,"[2] and to me, that seems quite significant. How significant? Well, the Surgeon General of the United States sees loneliness as a public health concern, equating its mortality impact to smoking 15 cigarettes a day.[3]

So, yeah—I'd say it's a problem.

But the issue is much worse than surface-level gloom or a widespread individualistic spirit among the youthful masses. In reality, we are experiencing an epidemic of loneliness and isolation. And surprisingly enough, the self-prescribed remedies that young people regularly use to deal with feelings of detachment often fall under the same categories. In our search to alleviate the pain of loneliness, I've found that the crutches we use end up being hazardous and creating more problems, not fewer.

The Future Can Be Bright

But I want you to know that there is hope! Life can always do a U-turn—things can change from dark despair and loneliness to profound joy and connection in legitimate relationships with others. If you're currently experiencing loneliness like Natalie, Josh, Sam, and Malika, it doesn't have to stay that way.

I want to tackle some of the issues that I've seen come up time and time again—the things that we hold onto for comfort yet actually cause us pain. But for each false promise, I will give you a bright promise to take its place—an authentic solution for healing that will practically and tenderly guide you toward community, friendships, and a genuine passion for what it means to live a fulfilling life alongside Jesus Christ. Loneliness is attempting to destroy our ability to connect with God and others in a way that helps us to thrive, so we are going to explore solutions that go after the roots of feeling detached.

I care deeply about your generation, and I've seen what loneliness can do to young people who are suffering from it—young people who hate it, and want to know what they can do about it. And because of this, the coming chapters will be full of a lot of straight talk about what I see going on and how you can be super intentional about not just addressing your surface-level loneliness problems but your root-level loneliness problems too.

I've always personally responded well to verses like Proverbs 3:11-12, which says, "My son, do not despise the LORD'S discipline, and do not resent his rebuke, because the LORD disciplines those he loves, as a father the son he delights in." Going after the root problems in life can feel quite uncomfortable and even painful at times, because it's digging deep into our lives. But when the digging is done in love and not harshness, we can know it's for our good. So, I'm going to attempt to unearth the roots out of a motivation to love and care for you.

If a tree is producing rotten fruit on its branches, the temptation is to pick off the bad fruit and hope the tree generates good fruit next season. But if you want more than just fingers crossed for a better crop next year, you get wise and prune off the bad, dead things and add in the good, life-giving things to address the real problem at the deepest levels.

Likewise, our temptation with life's problems is to deal with the symptoms of what's going on and wish for the best afterward. But to find genuine solutions to the problem of loneliness in our lives, we must ask better questions about why we're experiencing these feelings of detachment.

We have to get to the deep levels and apply lasting good news that will generate real and enduring change. Jesus is the friend, brother, and Savior who is the only unwavering answer to our loneliness problem, and I intend to show you how he can thoroughly and practically change your life. Then you'll have more than hope when dealing with your loneliness problem—you'll have confident gospel assurance.

PART ONE:

Screen Time

CHAPTER 1

Deepening the Disconnect: Digital Identities

You probably already know this, but an online social life isn't super social. Think about it: if you see a group of people all huddled together at a bus stop with their collective heads bowed, it might look as if they're praying together—but more than likely, they're all scrolling on their individual phones.

At its inception, social media and the digital world was created to make life more convenient and communal for people all over the world to connect. But now we can see that it's actually proven to have the adverse effect on the majority of people (young and old alike!) who use it regularly. It hasn't really connected us more closely with people; in some cases, it's driven us apart.

Of course, it's not all bad. One of the primary ways I keep in touch with some people in my life is through my phone—albeit by direct messaging funny memes and videos while never typing an actual word—but I'm attempting to communicate nonetheless. The upside to your generation having a nearly universal engagement with technology in everyday life since you were kids is the ability to connect with people all over the globe, to gain a broader perspective on an endless number of topics, and to keep in touch easily with friends who aren't close by. We have the internet to thank for those good things!

Connecting with others through your phone in moderation can be awesome, but I believe that one of the primary explanations for why you might be experiencing loneliness and isolation is because of this constant access to the online world. I've seen dangerous addictions start early because parents gave their third- and fourth-graders unlocked smartphones, allowing their kids unfettered access to video games, porn, and other dopamine-inducing digital vices. Maybe this was your experience as a kid, and it created tons of problems and addictions for you later in life. If so, you get what I'm talking about.

Even if your parents were adamant about not giving you a phone or iPad when you were younger, technology will still have left its mark because it's so much a part of our culture. Regardless of how poor the average 20-something is today, I've never met one who doesn't have some kind of a smartphone. It's almost impossible to think about not having a phone because of the adoption of technology by practically everyone, everywhere, all the time.

Hardware and software advancements have given us opportunities to feel grafted into digital communities in ways that we would never experience if we didn't plug ourselves in. Your individual accounts, memes, gifs (no matter how you pronounce that word), emojis, Memojis, avatars, profile pics, and handles all provide you with access to the communities you want to communicate with. Your digital identity has generated a way for you to express yourself and relate to others in the world.

We believe it has given us something that will help us digitally link arms with others in community, but has it? All those young people at the proverbial bus stop I mentioned at the beginning of this chapter might think that they're staying connected, but they're not really present with one another. So here's the important question for you to ask yourself: has your digital presence really connected you or has it made you experience greater degrees of detachment from others?

You might be cool with the digital connections you currently have. You feel and experience a great sense of belonging in whatever corner of the digital social sphere you've adopted. You're good. Or maybe you're keenly aware of the dangers our phones and technology pose to any human being looking to connect, so you've always been cautious about how much and how often you check your phone. Or perhaps you're somewhere in between, not giving much thought to the consequences (bad or good) of including technology in your everyday life.

Regardless, I believe the irony in all of this digital "connection" is that we've detached from others more than we've joined others in our desire to plug in and belong. And as a result, you may be experiencing an increasing sense of solitude as you dive deeper into your phone in escape or in search of a network you'll never be able to find.

Why? Because you're looking in the wrong place.

Fake It

Does your digital identity—your online profiles and how you present yourself online—make you feel more like yourself or less? You know that every post you see on social media, as well as the ones you make, is edited content. You know that if you record yourself, it's going to be from an angle that's probably the most flattering view of your face. You'll cut out that part at the end of the video when you blink and the recording pauses to make you look like an MMA fighter after several rounds of taking a beating. Yes, what you put out online is you—but it's the shined-up edition of you, because hiding the untidy or ugly parts of yourself is what has to happen if you want to be accepted as confident, attractive, intelligent, and capable to whoever is looking.

Bottom line: you know this isn't the real, raw you. But we see that this strategy works for other people whose followers, subscribers and likes keep growing when they show the best polished (not fully real) version of their lives. Even accounts that aim to show a more unkempt authenticity include a careful curation of what's fit to be shown and leave out anything they'd find genuinely embarrassing. Online influencers create a brand that needs to be nurtured and edited to an ambiguous list of specifications, and if they don't, their online "community" is going to abandon them for someone flashier, prettier, funnier, or more extreme. I can't help but think there must be a nagging little voice behind the library of content that knows they're hiding behind a constructed version of themselves. So, are their online connections genuine if they're not really interacting honestly?

As we scroll through our feeds and deliberate about what we should post next, we know we can be dropped or unfollowed at any moment if someone better comes along. We know our digital platforms are volatile and unsteady ground to build our lives on, and that creates a deep sense of insecurity. Being unfollowed can feel a bit like a breakup with a boyfriend or girlfriend—often a soul-crushing rejection of relationship.

The hunger for legitimate relationship that constantly grumbles in the belly of your soul isn't really being fed through the creation of a digital identity because you need something true. Let me run with this metaphor for a minute...

Gas-Station Snacks

Your soul wants and needs the nourishment of real food. Real connection. Real relationship. Real people. And you'll only get fed the food you need for growth and health when you experience the genuine article—real community.

But if you're feeding your soul with a steady stream of digital relationships with others whom you don't really know and who don't actually know you, you're essentially cramming convenience store snacks down your throat all the time to assuage the hunger. Sure, if you're on a real-life road trip and need to stop at a gas station to fuel up and grab a soda, some candy, and a bag of Doritos, it's fine—as long as you don't do that for every meal of every day. If you do, you're going to eventually become very unwell from lack of nourishment to your body.

Again, I'm not saying all digital communication is bad, so don't get me wrong. The online world can be useful and fun. It doesn't always fall into the category of "detrimental." But your digital profile interacting with other digital profiles out there via apps isn't the real you interacting with the real versions of other people. Digital connection—be it through streaming services, parasocial relationships, online forums, or scrolling social feeds—is essentially throwing junk food into a hungry soul that aches for real nourishment. The convenience of convenience store nibbling will starve you because hearty, satisfying connection is what you really need. You need to know and be known.

So, what's the solution? Is it simply putting down your phone, going out there, and making a bunch of friends with people in the real world? Maybe.

But here's the thing: relying on a digital identity isn't necessarily the root problem. It's a crutch—a facade hiding the real issue going on under the surface of your life. I think the growling in your soul is further down and further in than finding a solution in the motherly advice of "Go make some new friends, sweetie." Truly knowing and being known comes in a relationship that can't be replicated by any other relationship in the universe—a relationship with the living God. It's one of a kind, and it alleviates the hunger once and for all.

That being said, it's also true that we are meant to experience real closeness, care, and truth through other people so that we can better understand the love, grace, and fatherly heart of God. Making friends certainly isn't a lame consolation prize, and I'm willing to bet that if you picked up this book, you might want real help in forming warm, real, strong relationships with people as well as with God.

So don't worry—we'll get to both of these things.

Reflection Questions

1. Has your hunger for legitimate relationships influenced the way you use technology and social media? In what ways have you pursued online connections with people to the neglect of your relationships in the real world?

2. Have you ever experienced feeling that others know things about you but they don't really know you? What was that experience like?

3. Have you personally experienced digital relationships as being like junk food to your soul? What do you think are some characteristics of relationships that are actually soul-nourishing?

CHAPTER 2

Authentic Healing: Gospel Grasp

"Now this is eternal life: that they know you, the only true God, and Jesus Christ, whom you have sent."

(John 17:3)

I'm a military kid. My stepdad was in the air force for 30 years, and when I was younger, my life was characterized by constantly moving to new locations. We went from California, where I was born, to North Dakota, then to Guam (that tropical island out in the Pacific Ocean), and then to Virginia for an abnormal stint of four years in one place. But once my sophomore year of high school rolled around, we moved again to Montgomery, Alabama.

When my family and I first arrived, my parents made the decision to put me and my sister in a private Christian school. Now, this school's students were not what you would call "super welcoming." In fact, this Christian school didn't give Christianity a good name at all—a lot of the kids were incredibly mean to me for no apparent reason. It was hard to be the new guy, and I found that for the first few weeks, I only had one other dude to hang out with—another new kid, ironically named Christian.

Christian and I sat at lunch together every day for those first few weeks of tenth grade, until one day when I showed up at our regular spot in the cafeteria for lunch—and Christian wasn't there. I quickly scanned the room and saw him sitting with most of the other guys from my grade at a different table, with no room for me to join.

My stomach churned a bit, so I sat down and looked at him every now and then as I started to eat my lunch in our regular spot. Only this time, I was by myself. I caught him occasionally making brief eye contact with me and then looking away with obvious guilt each time.

I sat at the end of that cafeteria table with literally nobody else. It was like a movie in which the camera pans up and away through the room to an overhead shot of me sitting all alone, flanked by several other, completely full lunch tables crammed with chattering high-schoolers eating their food.

Now, I'm not all that young anymore, but you are, so I'd bet you can easily remember that the time you least want to be flying solo in high school is during lunch. Right? I can still feel the sour anxiety in my stomach right now as I think about what I experienced that day all those years ago.

It was horrible—and everyone else in the room knew it too. So much so that after about eleven or twelve excruciatingly long minutes, one of the girls from my grade came over and invited me to sit with some other girls at her table for the rest of lunch. I took her up on it, but the damage was done.

This was just an eleven- to maybe twelve-minute moment from when I was 15 years old, and I can still remember every detail of that short time with remarkable clarity. It still hurts because it's burned into my mind, soul, and spirit. But the question is: why?

As I've thought about this sporadically over the years (and honestly, as I've talked about it with my counselor), I've come to this conclusion: it still hurts decades later because I felt a deep sense of loneliness.

Dark Corners

Isolation is something that sticks. If I gave you a few minutes to pause and think about a time when you felt the most lonely, isolated and detached—all by yourself—it probably wouldn't take you long to come up with stories from your past or present, and the consequential emotions when you went through those times.

Loneliness is pretty awful, right? But why is it awful? Why is it so terrible when we feel cut off and all alone in our dark corners (whether that be figuratively online or literally in the real world)? Well, as you search the Scriptures, they give you an answer: it's because you and

I were made to be meaningfully connected. God declared that it was "not good" for us to be alone (Genesis 2:18). Did he mean that we should be connected with purpose to other people? Sure—and we'll get there.

But your desire for connection and community comes from the God who made you "in his own image" (1:27), and it can therefore only be met in God himself. It all starts with him. A deeper understanding of who you are in relation to your heavenly Father begins to heal the deep loneliness you may be experiencing both online and in real life.

The likes will never add up to enough. The compliments in the comment section can never applaud you enough. The hearts on your messages can never satisfy you enough. Your carefully curated digital identity will never appease your desire for genuine connection because that connection can only be met in a relationship with God through his Son.

And the more you know him, the more you truly understand that you are known at the deepest level possible. You are loved more than you could ever imagine. Your hunger to be genuinely connected and accepted is perfectly met in the person of Jesus Christ.

Real Connection

The only reason why any of us could ever experience this kind of community and relational connection with God is because of Jesus himself. Our sin fractured the connection with God in the first place and Jesus is the one who gives us the opportunity to be meaningfully connected to our Creator.

How? Because on our behalf, he was purposefully disconnected:

> *God made him who had no sin to be sin for us, so that in him we might become the righteousness of God.*
> *(2 Corinthians 5:21)*

What does that mean? Well, the entire reason why Christians are able to experience meaningful connection with God the Father is because Jesus the Son at one point experienced the lack of meaningful connection with him. On the cross, Jesus was isolated and detached from his Father (Matthew 27:46) so that we could be accepted by the Father. He was cut off for a time so that we could be grafted into the family of God and Christian community. He was denied and rejected by his friends when he needed them most so that we could be called friends of God (John 15:15; James 2:23).

He experienced the ultimate loneliness when he was crucified for our sins and cosmically separated from God for the first time in all of eternity. He was cast out of communion with God so that we could be welcomed into fellowship with the one who made us. He was excommunicated from the family so that we could be adopted into his family and counted as daughters and sons (Galatians 4:4-7).

Before Jesus came, we all were in a state of separation from God; our sins had "hidden his face" from us

(Isaiah 59:2). But he was separated and became sin for us while on the cross so that we could experience the uniqueness of Christian unity with God the Father and with each other (1 Peter 3:18). Because of Jesus, we can experience the authentic healing of genuine connection that everyone is looking for out there in the digital world.

Because of his sacrifice on our behalf, we can taste meaningful connection, purposeful depth, quality relationships, and familial intimacy. That connection with God was made possible by the sacrifice of Jesus of Nazareth—our disconnected connector.

Jesus makes everything we've been talking about possible because of his perfect life, death, resurrection, and ascension. Our meaningful connection as believers is only possible because of the sacrifice Jesus made for us when he took the penalty we deserve because of our active rebellion and passive indifference toward God. Then, he sealed loneliness's death when he rose from the grave and conclusively killed our detachment from God forever. It's all about Jesus.

For anyone who admits their own sin and need for Christ, and then believes in Jesus as their perfect sacrifice and true ruling authority, they are rescued by God for all eternity. They come into a relationship with their Creator, and loneliness can become a memory from the past. They are given the gift of God's Spirit to help them live the Christian life and become more and more like Jesus over time. They are invited into the ultimate community as a child of God amongst

God's people, and nothing is ever the same. Life for the Christian is truly never lived in isolation because God himself dwells within every born-again believer.

This is the gospel, and only a Spirit-gifted relationship with Jesus Christ will satisfy our craving to know and be known. The verse I highlighted at the beginning of this chapter, John 17:3, is part of Christ's prayer for us and communicates that he knows exactly what we need—a genuine, life-giving connection with our Creator and Sustainer, along with a godly community where he wants us to thrive.

Yes, I may have been alone and rejected by my friend at the lunch table that day back in high school, but because of Jesus, I know I am always welcome at the greatest table, accepted and seated with Christ. A life in Christ is a life with Christ, and when you're with another person—a person who loves you enough to sacrifice himself for you—by definition, you're never alone.

I think this is one of the most misunderstood aspects of the Christian life, which needs more attention—when you're a Christian, whatever you may go through, you are never truly isolated. You are always connected to the lover of your soul. His posture toward you in your weakness, insecurity, loneliness, and fear is always one of warmth, care, concern, empathy, and unconditional love. He calls you his friend, his child, his beloved—he's absolutely wild about you!

In the book of Romans, the author Paul says, "He who did not spare his own Son, but gave him up for us all—how will he not also, along with him, graciously give us all things?" (Romans 8:32). This means that even though you have rebelled against him, God paid the ultimate price to bring you back to himself. And that ultimate, extreme benefit-above-all-benefits comes with countless other privileges too, including peace, security, and satisfying contentment. In the gospel, he offers us love for who we truly are—we are both fully known and fully loved. The floor will never drop out from under us, and the ultimate soul-crushing rejection will never come, because "he will never leave you nor forsake you" (Deuteronomy 31:6).

If you are someone who hasn't heard that before, or you're kind of scratching your head at the idea of this meaningful connection, the very first step toward this kind of togetherness is saying yes and accepting the payment God has offered to make on your behalf in Jesus' life, death, and resurrection. A yes to his sacrifice for you is the first step into the kind of community that will ultimately last forever because it'll go on into all of eternity.

Admit first that you need it—that you need him. And as you adopt a humble posture of seeking God's grace, he will always move toward you with overflowing joy, welcome, and comfort. Psalm 72:12-13 says, "For he will deliver the needy who cry out, the afflicted who have no one to help. He will take pity on the weak and the needy and save the needy from death." He wants to connect you with himself.

Regardless of where you're at right now—how mature in faith you may feel, where you're at on the socioeconomic scale, or how much of a moral failure you are—let me tell you that you were made for meaningful connection and community, starting with God and then branching out to others too. And sometimes God actually woos people to himself and teaches them about meaningful relationships through others first, making the gospel plausible and a relationship with him a reliable reality.

So, even though it can be daunting, move toward him, and you'll find a truly different way of living than what you've perhaps settled for in your digital identity. Move toward him, and you'll find a more fulfilling and abundant way of life. Jesus says of his followers:

> *I have come that they may have life, and have it to the full. (John 10:10b)*

Gospel-Grasp How-Tos

Okay, let's get super realistic with this. You may be new to this, or you may have been a Christian for a while but grown more distant from Jesus, so in terms of practicality, I want to give you a couple of how-tos that you can apply right now as you ask the question: so what am I supposed to do?"

1. Ask God to engage your heart

Sometimes in life, we don't feel like moving toward God. Maybe we're upset, frustrated, angry, or even apathetic when it comes to how we feel about him, and it can be a real struggle when our heart isn't engaged or tender towards the Lord. Frankly, you may not even want to engage with, understand, or have a better grasp on the promises of the gospel sometimes! But, do you want to want to? And if you don't want to want to know Jesus more fully (this may sound silly at first), don't you want to want to want to?

Whatever may be going on with you right now, try to find your rock-bottom base level of desire for God, and when you're there, ask him to engage your heart and stir an affection for him in your life that you haven't experienced before.

Not everyone is ready to dive in in a way that matches the enthusiasm of others, so take an honest look at where you happen to be right now and keep asking God to engage your heart in ways that you simply cannot manufacture on your own.

2. Dig into Scripture in anticipation that he'll meet you there

There's a lot of Christian advice that settles on "pray and read your Bible more," and sometimes that can be eye-roll-inducing. However, I once had an older friend of mine say to me, "There will come days in your walk with God when you won't want to read your Bible, but go ahead and do it anyway. There are plenty of times when I don't feel like flossing my teeth, but I do it because, even though I may not feel like keeping up with my oral hygiene, it's the best thing for me." Now, I don't know about your flossing routine, but I think listening to God is infinitely more important than removing tartar build-up. Immersing yourself in Scripture is vital to the health of your soul, and you get the opportunity to take in the actual words of God when you read the Bible.

Hearing from him through his word is a very real way of meeting with the Creator of the universe, and it's a privilege many believers (myself included!) neglect. But a thriving relationship with God is what we were made for, and time in the Bible fosters genuine connection with him. It's how we get to know him, his character, his love, and his desires for us as his children. We literally meet with him when we study his word (both independently and corporately), and a relationship with God gives the greatest sense of community we can experience.

In the Bible, we learn and understand more about the person of Jesus, how he interacts with other people, and what he teaches about the kingdom of God. We see how he transcends religious teaching and urged the people of his time—and urges us—to come to him and find rest for their weary souls. We observe and understand that in him is abundant life because he wants us to have a personal relationship with him. This isn't about box-checking or religious activity to try and appease him. Instead, it's about intentionally putting effort into the greatest relationship you and I could ever have. In his word, we can plumb the depths of the gospel and develop a firmer grasp on the magnitude of what Jesus did for us, helping us go further up and further in when it comes to our relationship with God.

When we try to get rid of loneliness and have our needs met by digital substitutes, they will always be junk-food solutions to serious spiritual nutrition problems. When our spiritual stomachs rumble with hunger to connect, a greater grasp on the gospel and turning to Jesus to meet that need will help us address our loneliness problem in the best possible place—at the heart level.

Reflection Questions

1. How could a daily grasp on the reality that Jesus was disconnected for you—so that you could be connected to God—potentially impact your everyday life?
2. In what ways are you currently moving toward God? Think of specifics.

If you've never made the initial decision to say yes to the relationship God offers you in Jesus Christ, take the time right now to admit your need for God to rescue you from your sin. Confess your desire to be a part of God's family and to follow Jesus. Ask him to meet you in your brokenness and loneliness and to help transform and cleanse you. By faith, receive the gracious gift of new life and restored relationship that he offers to you in the person and work of Jesus, and then confidently rest in the fact that you are forever a child of God. Take a moment to pray right now before you move on to something else and become distracted by other people, places, and things. It all starts by starting with him.

PART TWO:

Relationship

CHAPTER 3

Deepening the Disconnect: Porn and Casual Sex

"Whoever isolates himself seeks his own desire;
he breaks out against all sound judgment."

Proverbs 18:1, ESV

Picture with me for a second a typical corporate manager, dressed professionally, sitting at a big boardroom table across from a man in a suit who looks as if he's just been told his dog died. The manager looks at the downtrodden man and utters the phrase, "It's not personal—it's just business."

When people use this expression—inside or outside of a boardroom context—they're usually trying to defend themselves. They want you to know that they're working on the basis of cool logic and fact, and that feelings shouldn't intertwine themselves with business matters.

In other words, there's no personal connection—this relationship is purely transactional.

I believe that as we look at the sexual aspect of our cultural landscape right now, much of its general attitude comes from the same sentiment: it's not personal—it's just business. Maybe you've heard things like this before:

> *"Watching porn isn't that big a deal. Everyone does it. At least I don't have to worry about STDs or pregnancy."*
>
> *"I have needs, she has needs, and we're getting those needs met whenever we hook up—feelings don't need to be involved."*
>
> *"I want fun but without the commitment, so porn gives me that."*
>
> *"We're not in a relationship; it's just sex."*

Okay, maybe you're thinking that people don't usually voice this stuff out loud, but trust me when I tell you that being in college ministry for a while has given me tons of opportunities to hear all kinds of reasons that non-believing (and Christian) young people come up with to justify why they should be allowed to have casual sex and/or watch porn whenever they want. When the accepted norm within a culture is putting your own desires and needs above anything or anyone else, thought patterns like those you just read above are the fruit of that norm.

But when this view of sex sinks down into the deepest levels of our belief system as a culture, symptoms begin to reveal themselves in disturbing ways. Yeah, commitment-free sex and porn use are the symptoms, but equally as bad is just how lonely people become when their sexuality is transactional—not personal but just business.

By Design

When you go all the way back to Genesis 2, you'll see pretty quickly how God designed the sexual aspect of life to be between a husband and a wife. Adam and Eve were sharing themselves with one another sexually, and there was absolutely zero shame involved (Genesis 2:23-25). It might be difficult to imagine, but sex wasn't originally created to be "naughty," "nasty," or "obscene." Just the opposite, actually.

And because God created it as a way for a husband and wife to connect with one another on a deeply intimate level, sex was designed with the intention of being a reflection of the intimacy a person can have with God himself. It was invented by God to deepen connection in a safe, committed relationship (like the one a Christian has with him).

It isn't just biological or mechanical—sex is emotional, vulnerable, and incredibly spiritual. It's designed to be personal in every way: invented by the personal God, who created personal people to share within the context of a personal covenant relationship. It's the very proof of closeness and connection.

But what happens when this good design for sex feels out of reach? What happens when our desire to rid ourselves of loneliness finds another faulty crutch to lean on?

Porn Use

It's no secret that when someone feels unloved and unknown (for whatever reason), watching porn can be a huge temptation. Why is that? Because porn promises to alleviate the negativity of feeling unwanted and detached from others. It's a very now-based pseudo-solution that gives the user a quick hit of pleasure, which is often what we look for when we're in pain. Some people watch porn to find pretend acceptance or satisfaction when they feel rejected, inadequate, or lonely. Some watch it to feel a sense of comfort when everything else in the world feels cold, unapproachable, or dangerous.

So, if someone who is hungering to connect and be known can opt for a momentary shortcut to ease the pain of isolation by watching porn, the shortcut is going to be profoundly tempting. Pornography use paired with masturbation sparks a false sense of connection internally, and that spark is addictive. In fact, I have a friend, Ben Bennett, who is the founder of a sexual wholeness ministry, and he shared some research with me that's fascinating. He found out that, in the same way most addictions work, watching porn releases a high level of dopamine in the brain, causing a euphoric feeling of pleasure.[4] Over time, however, watching porn can lead to fixed neurological pathways in the brain,[5] and as a result for many, it becomes an addiction that's extremely difficult to break.[6]

Similar to what happens with a drug, tolerance builds up in the brain after a person repeatedly views pornography,[7] and consequently that leads to a desire for more explicit and taboo forms of porn—plus a desire to watch more and more. Maybe you know someone who has experienced this, or maybe this has been your personal story—if so, I want to help (and will aim to in the coming chapter). But if this isn't what you've been through, please don't switch off, because this section could really help you to understand the problem and be part of the solution in someone else's life.

The temporary high of porn use is often immediately followed by feelings of guilt and shame, and a general sense of ickiness. Why? Because, regardless of who you are or what you believe about God, your sexuality is incredibly sacred. We don't feel icky because sex itself is trashy; as we've seen, sex is glorious and personal. It's not just a function of the body; it's a profound part of who we are as people. So, when we injure and vandalize that deeply personal and important part of who we are with something like porn and masturbation, it's easy to immediately flip toward anguish and shame.

But it's important to say that the presence of shame and guilt is an indicator of the glory and weight of human sexuality. It's something we should notice with significance, not flippancy.

The science too is totally in line with the spiritual part of what I'm saying here. Studies have shown that things often quickly intensify and spiral as someone feeds their addiction. Consistent porn use leads to frontal lobe atrophy.[8] This affects the area of the brain that's responsible for impulse control, higher reasoning, and judgment. Over time, it can lead to a loss of control over behaviors and a lack of rational decision-making.[9] In other words, you're literally hurting yourself when you indulge in porn consumption.

But you might be thinking, "How can I be hurting myself with something so common as watching porn? It makes me feel good, not bad." Well, it's a classic case of "missing the forest for the trees," meaning you miss the bigger problem if you're focused on the smaller details. The self-harm of porn use leads to toxic stress, anxiety, depression, and other mental and emotional challenges.[10] It generates shame and makes us shrink away from community; and as we hide, we lose the opportunities we have to be known and loved, furthering our disconnection. And, in addition to loneliness, all of those things I just listed are pretty major epidemics in and of themselves.

So when you consider all the horrific ramifications of pornography use, and then think about God's original design for sex, porn becomes all the more grotesque. In fact, it's directly responsible for fueling the use and abuse of others, especially women in the industry who might be hurt, desperate, or even trafficked against their will. And as people become desensitized to porn, they begin viewing other human beings as mere commodities.[11] It teaches that people aren't really people and that sexual pleasure is to be taken, not given, crafting unrealistic expectations[12] for what sex is supposed to be.

Porn appears (on the surface) to be an escape from the hurt of isolation and loneliness, but just as with opioids promising to deliver physically injured patients from chronic pain, the "solution" ends up becoming more of a problem than the initial problem itself. Porn does nothing but harm the user, the user's relationships, and society itself. But if you're currently caught in this trap and finding it difficult to get out, please know that the gospel still applies directly to you. There is always hope in Christ, freedom from addictions when you're in a relationship with him, and a variety of resources written by insightful Christian authors who can help you get on the solution side of your struggles (see Appendix for specific recommendations).

"Casual" Sex

Porn can convince your brain that what you see on screen is what's supposed to happen in real life. Consequently, sexual feelings can be seen as an appetite to be satiated. If you're romantically involved with someone in any way, porn use generates the assumption that sex must be a factor in the relationship. The mindset that sex should be easy to get results in less satisfaction with life. Because porn use is so rampant, many people assume that sex should always be casual. But since it was never designed by God to be that way, the "casualness" of it will never produce the desired result.

Imagine a very expensive luxury watch. A timepiece like this wasn't made to be an instrument to drive nails into wood or drywall. If you try to use the expensive watch that way, the luxury piece itself is going to get annihilated. The watch was made for a different purpose than hammering nails, so to use it in a way that the designer never intended leads to brokenness and ruin.

Similarly, commitment-free sex (and other kinds of sexual experimentation that aren't technically intercourse) can often lead to less connection, not more. If you're following Jesus and want to be obedient to him, you probably know this already, but sexual activity of any kind beyond biblical boundaries has the tendency to drive a person toward disillusionment, disappointment, fear, guilt, and shame. Why? Because the kinds of connection and feelings you get from any kind of sexual activity with a person who isn't your spouse are actually really damaging.

I've seen this over and over again in college ministry with students who "just want to have a good time," and the good time quickly transforms into disconnection from others and a rampant feeling of being hurt and more alone. You were made for and deserve something better.

There's nothing casual about casual sex. The price tag for it is much higher than you think because the result isn't a breezy, pleasure-fueled life of liberation (as porn would have you believe). It's actually a shallow pursuit of erotic connection that traps someone in addiction and contempt for themselves and others. There's a reason why the journey home after a night of disconnected sex with someone is often called the "walk of shame." The label itself reveals that feelings of guilt and shame are common here. I'm not saying that's good (it's actually horrible to be labeled that way), but to a certain degree, even the broader culture we live in recognizes that casual and detached sex isn't a morally good thing.

So, what does this mean for you if you're a Christian who might be struggling in the area of porn use and sexual activity with others? Remember that you are first and foremost loved and forgiven by God—when you repent, he is always there with open arms of mercy. God is always up to something good, so when he's calling you to a life of sexual purity, he's calling you to just that: life. It's an invitation to something far greater than what the world says is awesome.

Is it difficult to take this path in our cultural climate? Will you feel like a complete alien among your non-believing friends because you draw boundary lines and they don't seem to at all? Sure. But life is never about the "liberation" of no boundaries. The invitation for a fish to jump out of the lake into the "freedom" of the air isn't an invitation to life at all. In this case, what looks like liberation is in fact suicide. True, rich, and fulfilling life isn't about no boundaries—it's about finding the right boundaries.

The right boundary for a fish is within water. And the right boundaries for human sexuality are found in

Scripture. Followers of Jesus shouldn't imitate the world because we believe that true life is found elsewhere: in Christ. If you're wrestling in this area (and statistically, you may be because 57% of young adults age 18-25 reported using porn monthly or more often[13]), don't settle for the brokenness the world offers when you can be satisfied in the one who made you to be satisfied by his living water (see Jeremiah 2:13).

Underneath It All

What we're looking for underneath all our sexual desires isn't something that can be found in fake, hollow, or pixelated pursuits. At the root level of our craving is once again an appetite for true connection. Real love. Genuine meaning.

This can only be found in the kind of bond that's created by the Creator of all things himself. Love is his invention—his idea—and when we enjoy it the way it was intended to be enjoyed, authentic connections and relationships are made.

Reflection Questions

1. In what ways have you treated sex and sexuality with the mindset of "It's not personal; it's just business" both toward yourself and toward others? How has that affected your feelings of loneliness?
2. Have you considered that porn use isn't ultimately self-pleasure but self-harm? After seeing some of the negative ramifications of

porn on users (lack of rational decision-making, toxic stress, anxiety, depression, other mental and emotional challenges, etc.), how is God working in your heart to turn you away from porn and its damaging effects?

3. Have you ever given much thought to the fact that love and sex are God's inventions? Does this way of thinking about them change your heart's approach to love and sex?

CHAPTER 4

Authentic Healing: Gospel Friendships

"A friend loves at all times."

Proverbs 17:17a

I love Jesus. I love my wife. I love my kids. I love sneakers. I love my dog. I love the fall season. I love Tostito's hint of lime tortilla chips. I love the NFL. I love the smell of freshly baked waffle cones. I could go on.

But "I love Scripture" and "I love chicken enchiladas" aren't talking about the same kind of love, even though I'm using the same word to describe how much I adore the Bible and also tomatillo-smothered corn tortillas stuffed with seasoned poultry. As you can see, not all loves are the same.

Yet often, when we hear the word "love" in our Western culture, our minds can immediately jump to the romantic, sexual kind of love (Greek word:

eros). It's natural to do this because of what our culture emphasizes loudly. If we hear, "Love is love!" we instinctively believe the conversation is focusing on the topic of romance and sex, not Mexican food.

But the Scriptures (and in particular, the New Testament) talk more about a different type of love—a brotherly kind of love, most often displayed within the context of close friendships (Greek word: *phileo*). Our definition of love can be quite small. God, however, expands our horizons when it comes to loving relationships, and can heal the hurts caused by porn use and casual sex when we discover and experience something only a Christian can enjoy: true gospel friendship and community.

Hear me out on this...

Community

Now, you may have read the title of this chapter and thought, "Why is he saying that gospel friendships are a way to heal from loneliness made worse by porn use and easy sex? That's kind of an odd remedy for a seemingly unrelated and powerful issue."

Well, maybe. But gospel friendships remind us in real time that there is a humanity to humans that will always be ignored by sexual activity beyond biblical boundaries—either casually outside of marriage or digitally in solitude. Viewing people as objects for sexual consumption is not uncommon for sinners like me and you (and nearly every other person who has ever lived), and the Bible confirms this when it says that our hearts are "deceitful above all things and beyond cure" (Jeremiah 17:9).

But rarely, if we're stuck in isolation, are we able to see that it's a bad thing to consume others. We are blind to our own blindness. But in the context of community that is able to be vulnerable with one another, others can help us to see. The Bible says that as believers, we make up the body of Christ (the church), and this body has many members (1 Corinthians 12:14). So it's vital that we are connected to the other members of the body and that they are connected to us in vulnerable community. We can't function properly as a Christian outside of those relationships with fellow believers, because following Jesus isn't about only the two of us. A hand that's disconnected from a body is pretty useless, so it makes no sense for us to try and go it alone, if you think about it. Being a Christian is being connected to other Christians. There's no other way because Jesus doesn't give us any other option.

So in light of that, are we asking authentic questions and giving honest answers when our friends and family inquire about our lives? Is there a continual spirit of truth among those who are closest to us? When honest, grubby, unfiltered authenticity reigns in our relationships, we can get real about our issues and then see God mold and shape us more into the image of his Son. God uses other believers to bring about real change, growth, and maturity in our lives.

The Bible says, "As iron sharpens iron, so one person sharpens another" (Proverbs 27:17). In other words, Christians have the ability to help other Christians become more godly Christians—that's how the body of Christ works. One author and pastor put it this way:

> *"Paul uses the picture of a body as the church, with Christ as the head. Now, think about how the body takes care of itself. I've got a head/brain that represents Jesus. If my left elbow decides that it itches, it sends up a message to the brain that says, 'I itch.' What does my brain do? My brain does not send magic brain-juice power down there to take care of the itch. Instead what it does is it signals my right hand and fingers and says, 'Hey, right fingers, brother left elbow has an itch; go take care of that.' And that's how the body works.*
>
> *"In the same way, when God has something that you are praying to him about doing in your life, he usually doesn't send down some magic power from heaven to fix it. What he does is he connects you to another person in the body of his church ... and that becomes the instrument through which he works in your life.*
>
> *"This means if you disconnect yourself from the church, you are disconnecting yourself from the power of God."*[14]

Gospel friendships help us understand and live out the Christian life in ways that would never be possible if we attempted to do it on our own. Godly church community provides the love, grace, strength, support, and presence that we need to thrive. Romans 12:4–5 says, "For just as each of us has one body with many members, and these members do not all have the same function, so in Christ we, though many, form one body, and each member belongs to all the others." In other words, we need other Christians to belong to as they belong to us.

Deadly Pools

Not long ago, my in-laws moved from their longtime home and downsized to a house that's closer to us but has a pool in the backyard. We were all so excited to visit them for the first time that summer. We even brought our dog with us (a little 20-pound/9kg cavapoo fluff-ball named Pippa) to play in the backyard while we all swam.

It was hot outside, so we put a bowl of fresh water down for Pippa, but she routinely ignored it and opted to drink instead from the swimming pool itself whenever she seemed to be thirsty. As I noticed her going back to drink from it over and over again, my father-in-law told me that the pool was kept clean through a combination of chlorine and salt water.

I didn't think this was healthy hydration for my little pup, so I went to go pick her up and put her inside the house. When I bent down to get her, she was in the middle of lapping up more salt water and chlorine, and as my arms wrapped around her mid-section, she growled and nipped at me. This was new behavior for our dog, so I verbally scolded her for attempting to bite me as I shut her inside the house. When I got back to the pool, my wife said with a breezy tone, "There's an illustration in there somewhere."

And my wife was right. You and I are just like my dog (stay with me on this).

We're searching for something out there on our own to satisfy our deep thirst in life. But when we think we've found something (like porn, compromise in the face of sexual temptation, letting things get as close to the edge as possible in a relationship, or even blatant sexual hook-ups) to ease the pain of our loneliness, we're actually lapping up salt water mixed with chlorine. We're going to pools of water that will never quench our thirst. In fact, those pools are actually killing us.

And when the grace of God through a community of gospel friends comes along (such as a healthy church family that we're involved with) and tells us that we're drinking salt water and chlorine, the temptation is to bite at the hands attempting to rescue us and say, "I'm fine! Leave me alone! I don't need your help!"

But if we're honest, we're probably not fine. God knows this, so he puts people in your life who care about you enough to love you in your mess and consistently point you to Jesus. He ushers in friends to create a safe space where you can bring your sins into the light so that you may be healed. He gives you fellow believers who get involved in your messiness and pull you away from what's destroying you.

And even if you do bite at the hands attempting to help you, believers who have experienced the life-changing power of Jesus know that a friend loves at all times (Proverbs 17:17a), regardless of how the other person responds in the moment. They have personally experienced the astounding grace of God in the gospel to the point that they are committed to being a godly friend. They are a humble, gracious extension of truth, even when that truth feels painful or annoying to face. A gospel friend can love you and simultaneously hold up a mirror to help you see your sin and its consequences. What may feel like an irritating intrusion in your life is a gift from God and tangible evidence of his grace.

God uses gospel friendships to help free us from the prison of sexual immorality. He uses gospel friendships to help us see others as human beings made in the image of God. He recalibrates our desires and draws us toward a community that loves us enough to not shy away from having the hard, honest conversations—but to also consistently point us to the one who heals and saves.

The Best Friend

Yes, we need gospel friendships in order to truly heal from the isolation caused by porn use and commitment-free sex, but you'll never ultimately be satisfied in your relationships with people until you've met and entered into a friendship with the ultimate person—Jesus Christ. Being in a relationship with Jesus doesn't guarantee that every other relationship you have will be satisfying, but your relationship with Christ will often affect the quality of your relationships with other people. He is the constant, in the midst of all of us unreliable people who will inevitably fall short at some point. He's the one who makes it possible for us to persevere in loving and being loved by unreliable failures. Let me explain...

The worst kind of relationship is the one you think you're in—but you're not actually in. Translation: there is no relationship if the other person isn't committed to the relationship.

If a guy believes he's in a romantic relationship with a girl but they're not actually dating because she's not into him, that's painful, right?

If a girl thinks she's part of a friend group but it makes fun of her behind her back on a separate text thread, it's hurtful, right?

But if you think you're in a relationship with God and you're playing house with him, you know a lot about him, you hang around enough with Christians to know the slang related to him, but you're not actually in a real relationship with him, it's not just painful or hurtful... it's tragic. Tragic on the level of eternal devastation.

This is particularly scary for me to contemplate because it was my tragic story for the first 19 years of my life. I was the quintessential "good kid" who never really rebelled against authority. In general, I did what I was told and checked all the right boxes when it came to ethical living. Consequently, I sincerely believed that God accepted me because he knew I was morally better than most other people in the world. Put plainly, I thought I could buy my way into God's favor through relatively righteous behavior.

But there are several problems that come with this kind of living, one of which is treating Jesus and a relationship with him like a boring to-do checklist. When your heart isn't connected to the "spiritual" activity you do, it's simply empty religion. The book of Proverbs says, "Above all else, guard your heart, for everything you do flows from it" (Proverbs 4:23). In other words, everything you are is an overflow of your heart, so if your actions aren't truly sincere when you perform religious activity, your religion isn't genuine.

More than likely, you understand this on a relational level with other people. Maybe you've experienced a friendship with someone where you just don't feel that their heart is fully engaged in the way yours is—there might be activities that you do together, but the other person is not truly committed as a friend. The relationship lacks the heart necessary to be an authentic connection.

And when it comes to how we relate to God, that dynamic is very similar. Doing religious things might mean you can label yourself, and get labeled by others, as a religious person, but if your heart isn't engaged in the things you're doing, there's really no true relationship there between you and God.

Just as standing in a garage doesn't make you a car, going to church or to a Bible study doesn't make you a Christian. So we all need to ask ourselves an important question: do we only know about God, or do we truly know him? It seems like a very subtle difference, but the difference itself has eternal consequences.

Up until I was 19, I knew a lot about God and even behaved obediently because I knew that he was real and probably watching me. Yeah, I was very "good," but I was terribly lost. I didn't actually have a relationship with God because I needed to repent of what theologian John Gerstner called, "my damnable good works."[15]

My goodness was getting in the way of knowing God as my ultimate friend. My goodness was preventing me from experiencing eternal life. My goodness was trying to earn God's grace. But if grace could be earned by being good, it would cease to be grace. So, I repented of my damnable good works, came to God in my neediness, and prayed that he would rescue me from myself. And when that happened, by God's grace, I entered into a relationship with him for the first time. No more empty religion—just unity with my Creator.

"But what about me?" you might be asking internally. You may have compromised in multiple ways with all that we've been talking about in these last two chapters, and you might be feeling a deep sense of shame and embarrassment because of your previous choices. Well, I have good news for you too: Jesus wants to be friends with you just as much as he wants to be friends with the "good" kids, like I was. If you're in a relationship with Christ, you are just as much forgiven, loved, and capable of change as any other follower of Jesus. And God will use gospel-focused friendships to help you change and become more of who you were always meant to be.

Connections like those between Christian friends are unmatched in this world when both people are committed to the lordship of Jesus Christ in their lives. Two random Christians might look different, come from different backgrounds, and be immersed in different cultures and drawn to different hobbies or interests, but if those two people have Jesus in common, the Bible says that they are spiritual siblings with each other and with Jesus (Matthew 12:48-50). Brothers and sisters in Christ. Relatives by the grace of God and the kindness of the Holy Spirit. They are unified in ways that go beyond this life, because those two people are going to spend eternity together with their Maker.

If your best friend is Jesus, the ultimate friend who truly loves you at all times (Proverbs 17:17a), then that means he loves you in every instance, without exception, constantly, continuously, perpetually, and uninterruptedly. Yes, even when some of your other friends might get tired of your repeated struggles and give up on you. Even when you're disgusted with yourself and hate that you keep falling into the same sexual sin over and over again. Jesus loves you when you feel unlovable. And the gospel friendships you share with others will be the taste of heaven that helps free you from the slavery of isolation through porn use and casual sex. The ultimate friend, you'll find, will often meet you through his body of your fellow believing friends here on earth.

Gospel Friendship Tracks to Run On

You might be thinking, "I don't have any kind of framework to get the type of friends you're talking about or be the type of friend you're describing." If that's you, it's okay! Admitting that you're lacking and want things to change is a crucial first step.

So, here are a few suggestions about how to move toward and engage in gospel friendships in a way that helps you heal and helps the others around you heal too.

1. Start with prayer and ask God for the right kinds of friends

I remember a few years ago when I could honestly say that I didn't really have any good friends in my life who were willing to be vulnerably deep with me and also call me out on my sin and foolishness. I felt there was a big gap in my life at that time, so I prayed for God to give me some good, godly friends. It wasn't much more complicated than that, but I kept praying that prayer for a few months. And unsurprisingly, God gave me two really great, godly friendships unlike any I'd experienced before. One is a local church friend who I see in person regularly, and the other is a long-distance friend who I have a video call with once a month. Both friendships make me laugh, challenge me, point me toward Jesus by calling me away from my sin, and fill me with a ton of joy.

Yes, it can feel kind of obvious to pray and ask the Lord for godly, satisfying friendships, but don't skip this imperative step in your search for the right kinds of people you'd be pleased to call your friends. The adage "Talk to God about people before talking to people about God" can apply when it comes to sharing your faith but also in making some quality new friends—and don't be surprised if these friendships look different from the kind of friendships you expect.

2. Start viewing the opposite sex through the lens of friendship instead of sexualization

In a culture that sexualizes practically any and every close relationship, it can be really difficult not to view the opposite sex as someone or something to satisfy our own desires. Author and Bible teacher Jen Wilkin once said:

> *"The lie that has been told to a generation ... is that any intense feeling or strong feeling for another person—whether same sex or opposite sex—must have a sexual or romantic tone to it. The Bible says something very different."*[16]

She goes on to say that brother-and-sister relationships or brother-and-brother/sister-and-sister relationships exist in a non-sexual space, and if you extend that metaphor to the church, as the Bible does, viewing the opposite sex as brothers or sisters first is essential—and something that has to be recovered. "If not in the church," she asks, "then where?"[17] I believe Wilkin is right. Because sexualization or romanticization has become synonymous with any kind of strong feelings in our culture, it can be challenging to overcome the obstacle of thinking about anyone you enjoy from the opposite sex (or the same sex for that matter) as a potential romantic option. Consequently, we put man-made guard rails in place and quarantine ourselves off from either men or women for fear that we'll make each other stumble. Now, of course there needs to be discernment in how we interact as men and women, particularly for those who are married. Wilkin admits that intimate friendships with the opposite sex are not a good idea, but overall, I think you get the point. She further points out that too many restrictions can make the problem worse, not better. "Forbidding an entire category of relationships [with the opposite sex] actually sexualizes something that wasn't sexualized until the moment you forbade it."[18] And here's where Wilkin really zeroes in on the problem when it comes to the proper perspective on gospel friendships. If we view other people primarily as potential sex objects instead of primarily as potential friends, we'll fall into the traps of either regularly avoiding the opposite sex or regularly mentally drooling over the opposite sex. Over-sexualizing people is what produces a destructive culture of sex and porn use. And as we've already seen, the primary way God intends us to relate to one another is as a loving family.

3. Start thinking about how to put intentional effort into real-life friendships

Depending on what stage of life you're in, making friends can seem either super easy or ridiculously hard. When you're in high school or college, most people around you are heading in the same direction and operate on the same basic schedule. This is great! And it means there are lots of potential opportunities to make friends. However, when you graduate (either from high school or college), what once came easy now requires a lot of difficult work. There's quite a significant shift that happens in friendship when you move out of the education sphere, and you might feel a bit shellshocked if you haven't anticipated it. The energy that's required for making and keeping friends when you're in school isn't the same energy that'll be required of you later on in life if you want to make and keep friendships. So you're going to have to eventually try (sometimes harder than you're comfortable with) and put energy into forming friendships in a way that wasn't necessary when you were younger.

If you're intentional about the process of seeking out fellow Christ-followers in a local church that you're committed to, you'll have greater opportunities to find the right kinds of friends to share life with. Make time to intentionally eat meals with people. If you're going to work out, swap your headphones for a friend and talk to them while you lift or do cardio. Grab coffee, go for walks, study with each other, volunteer together... there are so many ways to apply this practically, so think creatively about how to build relationships into the normal routine of your life.

Start pursuing vulnerability in your friendships. The Bible tells us that the righteous choose their friends carefully (Proverbs 12:26), so picking the right kinds of friends to do life with is super important. I once heard my grandma say (and she probably ripped this off from somewhere else), "Show me a person's friends, and I'll show you an accurate picture of that person." Bottom line: the friends you choose will end up shaping who you are. If you constantly spend time around people who stick to surface-level conversation and never move deeper than jokes or small talk, you'll always feel hungry for something more profound in your friendships. And if you don't intentionally go deeper (either with current friends or new ones), shallow will become the norm, and you can end up lacking depth yourself.

You need vulnerability in your friendships—you need complexity, deep belly laughter, ugly cries, and raw honesty. You need trusted companions who are willing to graciously tell you the truth because they see sin in your life (sexual or otherwise) and love you enough to call you away from it—Proverbs 27:6a says that "wounds from a friend can be trusted." This may look like a small group of people you go deep with or just a couple of trusted friends who will always be there for you. Regardless, start pursuing the kind of friendship that's vulnerable on the level that makes you just a little bit scared because it's so genuine. Those are the kinds of friendships that will last and the ones that will reverberate throughout eternity.

I really hope this is the beginning of some help in the right direction. We need shoulders to cry on and the closeness of Christ-like friendship when we're hurt and in pain. We need gospel friendships to remind us of the truth and call us toward Christ-like living. We need accountability to help us live sexually moral lives that honor God, honor others, and honor ourselves. We need community to pull us away from isolation and the dangerous remedies we often opt for to alleviate our loneliness.

Reflection Questions

1. Where might God be using friends to call you away from attitudes or behaviors that are harming you? Do you think your friendships have the potential to go deeper and connect more vulnerably or bring challenge where needed?
2. Have you found yourself over-sexualizing the opposite sex in a way that can make it difficult for you to view others as friends? What personal perspectives need to change within you in order to move toward a more healthy, biblical way of viewing fellow Christians as brothers and sisters?

Take a moment right now and pray that God would provide you with the kinds of friends who care about you enough to call you toward godly living. Pray that he would, by his grace, lead you to the right kind of friends, who value their relationships with God more than anything else.

PART THREE:

Community

CHAPTER 5

Deepening the Disconnect: Polarization (Anger)

As much as we like to think that peer pressure is limited only to grade school, I'm sad to say that it spills over into pretty much every other part of life, regardless of age.

In high school, I was pressured into balancing a cafeteria chair on my chin during lunch. In college, I was pressured into pranking a campus ministry leader's front yard by sticking 4,500 plastic forks into their lawn. As a single dude in college ministry, I was pressured into going camping with a bunch of other guys out in the woods in the middle of winter (yuck). And as a young dad, I was pressured by my kids to stream episode after episode of truly awful children's programming when all I wanted to watch was football.

Over the years, I've come to the realization that it'll probably never go away.

"Would you like to round up and donate $0.68 to the environmental education nonprofit that builds beehives near corporate office buildings in southeast Pennsylvania?" the cashier asks me a little too loudly as I'm aware of the line of people behind me at the grocery store, staring at the back of my head.

I have no desire to do so, but I mumble, "Uh... sure," to avoid any judgment from the others who also heard. This is peer pressure. (Side note: This exact question was never really asked of me, but you get my point.)

And believe it or not, we're all experiencing a steady stream of the same thing as we engage with people in the real world and online.

Pick a Side

"What side are you on?" is a common underlying (if not overt) question asked in the digital world of late, whether it be about celebrity romances gone bad, politics, social justice issues, or a variety of other hot and dividing topics. The assumption that it's one or the other is forcing a sense of polarization onto anyone who dips their toes into digital news outlets or video clips (fed to you by the best algorithms and AI in the world). The "either/or" mindset is prevalent practically anywhere you go—both online and in real life—and the push (peer pressure) to choose one side or the other is fairly strong.

And sure, hastily picking a team might alleviate the discomfort of not belonging—we all naturally want to feel included with a group of people—but the consequential byproduct of feeling the push to one side or the other is generating anger and loneliness. Here are a few examples...

When Julia was walking on campus at the beginning of her freshman year, she was stopped by someone on the quad and asked point blank, "Are you a conservative or a liberal?"

"Neither," she responded but was then promptly told she should pick the more conservative side when it came to her vote in the upcoming government election. Julia tried to politely disagree and keep walking but was told (not so delicately) that if she didn't vote "correctly" in the election, it put the country at risk and that she needed to take her vote seriously—either she was for freedom or against it.

Dan is a student I met and was discipling for two years. During our times together each week, I noticed that he was growing more and more irritated by political content in the news apps he viewed multiple times a day. The social-media stories he posted were an obvious clue that he wasn't pleased with any decisions of the government in office at the time. Over lunch one day, Dan got fired up and complained to me that every decision the president made was awful, dangerous, and stupid. I attempted to steer him towards trust in the sovereignty and good shepherding of God despite any issues in the country's leadership. But our 60-minute time together was no match for his constant scrolling down the rabbit hole, as the algorithm fed him video after video about the inept presidential administration.

Dan admitted that several weeks into absorbing this one-sided content, he felt himself getting angrier and angrier at the "other side," which (according to the videos) would be responsible for the downfall of Western civilization as we know it.

Robin was a fan of a Christian YouTuber who taught apologetics, took on head-first the false teachings of the secular culture, and gave good biblical perspective on a variety of subjects. But Robin noticed that within the last year or so, this content creator became increasingly polarized against "other" Christians who didn't draw the same kind of definitive lines that he did over hotly contested issues.

Sensing a growing hostility on the part of the YouTuber, Robin became confused but trusted him because of his previous thoughtful, intelligent, and seemingly Christ-centered perspectives on so many subjects. His views and subscriber numbers were clearly going up the more one-sided his opinions, so Robin figured he must be doing something right by calling out other Christians who seemed to allow the ungodly secular culture to shape their faith.

Several months later, Robin found herself progressively more upset with other believers who didn't share the same perspectives that she and her now favorite

YouTuber held. After a few heated arguments with others in her campus ministry, Robin decided to leave the ministry she had been a part of for two years in favor of another campus organization that "wasn't afraid" to talk about what she felt was most important. She abandoned her closest friends because she believed they were on the wrong side.

Inauthentic Community

Maybe you read these examples and think, "Okay, some people might buy into that kind of extreme thinking, but I'm not naive enough to be swayed into one kind of camp or another."

Or maybe you're someone who has placed many stakes on hills because you have no problem living in a camp that "stands up for the truth" no matter what the consequences are.

Regardless, I think it's safe to say that in our present time, two-sided debates continually wash in like waves on a shoreline, so it's easy to choose an echo chamber of people who share the same ideals as you, however mild or extreme. Plus, being collectively angry at someone else, another tribe, or an opposing belief system gives a group of like-minded people an emotional rise and breeds the perception of greater unity.

But if you do engage with a group that rallies around a particular ideal or goal, would you consider the possibility for a minute that the community you're part of may not actually be as genuine as you think?

Why am I asking? Because the foundation of a polarized group is usually built on loyalty to the ideal—not the relationships within the group. In other words, all the relationships revolve around a specific opinion itself rather than the actual people who hold said opinion. Consequently, angry polarization gets hyped up more and more while genuine connection with other people erodes.

Another example might help here. There is a famous music artist who used to preach body positivity through all her communication channels and under the spotlight on stage. Admittedly overweight herself, she would lecture anyone who would listen, demanding that society should accept larger people and not ask them to change because they are perfect just the way they are.

However, when this musician ended up losing a lot of weight herself, she was rejected and ostracized by the body-positivity community that she once publicly spoke for. It seemed pretty obvious that her "community" was more dedicated to their perspective than to her as a person or even as an artist.

Sadly, there isn't much community within a polarized community. So your time among the other people in the group (whether it be online or in person) not only isolates you from others with a different view but increases your sense of loneliness even within it. Deep down, you know that if you vocalized a different opinion from the one your tribe subscribes to, you'd be ostracized in a heartbeat. If you tried to "add a bit of gray" to the perspective that seems to be so black-and-white, you'd be quickly labeled a traitor to the group's shared values. And because that knowledge is there in your heart of hearts, you're aware that the people in your group only commune with you if you say and do the "right" stuff that they want you to say and do.

This kind of polarized group is a works-based group that requires your performance to maintain your status within it. No grace. No room for nuance. No believing the best. Just commitment to the idea. If you step out of line or waver at all on the idea, you no longer belong within the community.

Don't get me wrong: I'm not saying that every opinion-based group is crazy and bizarre. There are certainly healthy groups of passionate people working together for a cause or hobby that are positive places. But let's never forget that these groups of ideal-based people are never good substitutes for genuine Christian community.

Hold Up...

"Now wait a minute," you might object. "Aren't Christians themselves in a polarized group that claims to stand up for the truth whatever the consequences? Doesn't the Bible itself call us to pick a side when it comes to a lot of things we encounter in this world? How is biblical Christianity any different than what you're saying I should avoid?"

Good questions. Thank you for asking them.

I'll respond by asking: Does aligning yourself with what Scripture teaches make you more and more a humble, gentle, and respectful person, or does it simply make you feel angrier and more self-righteous? Is the Christian community you're a part of leaning on outrage because of what it's against or does it thrive on who and what it's for?

Polarized groups of people thrive on anger, fear, and pride in a way that identifies "the others out there" as the problem-makers in this world. But true Christianity teaches that your biggest problem in life isn't the other people out there but the sin that's inside your own heart. (See Jesus' words in Matthew 15:18-20.) And when you align yourself more and more with what the Bible teaches about sin, humanity, and the gospel, a posture of humility grows in your heart instead of a posture of outrage, anger, and cockiness.

Humility breeds more open ears and less of an open mouth. Humility shapes a person into someone who is "quick to listen," "slow to speak," and consequently, "slow to become angry" (James 1:19). Humility bonds you with others in a way that collective anger never could. Humility is the true fruit of following Jesus—not polarization, ostracization, and isolation. Humility leads to real relationships and authentic belonging.

So, does your church, campus ministry, group of Christian friends, or online Christian collective lead you more toward anger or humility? Being "narrow" isn't the issue. Every truth claim is narrow in one form or fashion. The real issue is: do "your people" make you want to sneer or look down on others? If so, your tribe might label themselves as Christian, but a group that sneers at others is not Christ-like and, therefore, is a poor representation of Christianity.

A great question to ask as you reflect on this would be: how does being a citizen of heaven (the literal good news of the kingdom) change my approach toward those who disagree with me, both inside and outside the family of God? There's a huge posture difference in that approach.

I urge you not to be wooed into a false sense of belonging (whether it be online or in real life) with a sneering group of people simply because you align with their perspective on something. If you find that the fruit of their perspective is polarization and anger, remember that human anger does not produce the righteousness that God desires (James 1:20). Instead, seek to genuinely belong to a community of fellow followers of Christ who exhibit the character qualities of humility toward others.

Non-Superglue

Connection within a polarized group might seem authentic at first because of how strong everyone's feelings are regarding the specific cause or passion, but what I'm trying to get across to you is that it's a counterfeit connection. You might feel that you belong in the group, but angry zeal for the cause is probably the only glue that's binding it together. And spoiler alert: it's not superglue or epoxy. In reality, it's frail because there's really no humanity (and certainly no godliness) in it if the other side must be dehumanized and brought down, and not respected or treated with kindness.

As we will see, the real glue that binds us to others is the Spirit of God working in our hearts to foster a gospel empathy we could not create on our own.

Reflection Questions

1. In what ways has peer pressure (both in real life and digitally via algorithms) played a part in the opinions you currently hold about potentially polarizing topics?
2. Regardless of your particular views, how has picking a side personally hurt or helped you?
3. In what ways does tribalism hinder genuine community? Do you have any examples, either personally or from another person?
4. Why do you think God calls us to a different kind of community—something that champions humility?

CHAPTER 6

Authentic Healing: Gospel Empathy

"Be kind and compassionate to one another, forgiving each other, just as in Christ God forgave you."

Ephesians 4:32

The first time I went to the dining hall at the beginning of my freshman year of college, there was a group of students picketing at the main entrance, walking in circles with soda cans tied to their ankles by string (for some reason). One girl was shouting into a megaphone, "It's not fair! It's not fair!" and holding up a sign that had a man's face with one of those big red circles around it and a diagonal slash mark across his head.

Even as a newbie freshman coming into a large and unknown university environment, I could have told you that yelling into the wind doesn't solve anything. There was nothing that they wanted anyone to sign or vote for; they weren't even explaining to people why they were upset. It was all just an angry presentation (or amazing prank—which with college students is always a possibility) to show people that this one guy was the problem.

Now, I don't have an issue with picketing or protests; I think it's great to exercise your right to free speech on a college campus. However, the way you go about communicating something is equally as important, if not more so, as the content of the message itself. And unless you're watching a movie that involves the Incredible Hulk, anger is repulsive. Sure, being overtly mad might get attention and multiple views online, and spark curiosity, but nobody wants to be around someone who's prone to outbursts or displays constant vitriol toward other people.

Proverbs 14:17a says, "A quick-tempered person does foolish things." Now, I might be wrong, but I don't think anyone wants to be around someone who acts like an angry fool. That kind of negative emotion pushes others away instead of welcoming them in. Someone with these negative character qualities repels others and prevents closeness in their life.

But I'm not being naïve here—I know there's plenty to be angry about when you look around at the world. With so much injustice, selfishness, and wrongdoing, the natural, knee-jerk reaction to all of that might be significant anger bubbling up in your mind and heart. There certainly is such a thing as righteous anger because, in many ways, the motivation that fuels righteous anger is love. But stomping and screaming to let out anger in a lack of self-control is not at all productive. If we find ourselves getting mad at a person or group, the reason for our anger is what we should be looking into.

Honestly though, sometimes getting angry feels really good—especially when you're alongside other people who are mad about the same thing that you are. But there's got to be a more robust, long-lasting solution to the problems we see and experience than simply pointing the finger elsewhere with a scowl on your face.

Where Do We Turn?

The gospel of Jesus Christ opens up the power for us to empathize with others in ways that wouldn't be possible without it. True empathy through the lens of the cross is the only heart-level solution to unification between two constantly arguing sides of the aisle.

Let's take the verse we started this chapter with and use it as a life example. Ephesians 4:32 tells us to be kind and compassionate, and to forgive one another as God in Christ forgave us. Sure, this sounds nice—when you're not angry and fired up. But when I'm enraged about someone or something, it feels impossible to weave kindness and compassion into my emotional tapestry, not to mention forgiveness. But maybe the apostle Paul is showing us here in his letter to the Ephesian church that we need the gospel to transform every part of us—even our seemingly unquenchable anger. The kind of heart that he's talking about sounds impossible to muster as a human being, but perhaps that's the point.

As Jesus himself said in Matthew 19:26, "With man this is impossible, but with God all things are possible." Admitting your neediness to God when it comes to anger is the beginning of heart transformation, because he is the one who changes hearts.

The gospel makes it possible for us to love our enemies as the Bible tells us to do (Romans 12:20-21). The gospel extinguishes the fires of rage that burn in people's hearts and transforms anyone who says yes to the power of Christ in their lives. The gospel can change anger into empathy in a way that nothing else in this world can. Let me share a personal example...

For the longest time, I could honestly say that I was mostly indifferent when it came to my relationship with my biological father. When I was around the age of thirteen, he pretty much stopped being interested in me—so I stopped being interested in him. For decades, I considered him to be an afterthought in my life that I simply didn't care about. Whenever mention of him did come up, though, I'd find myself agitated and angry at the idea of forgiving him or showing any kind of compassion. He was supposed to be the adult and not shut me out—why should I care about my father if my father didn't really care about me?

But a few years ago, the Holy Spirit began to work his way into the darker parts of my heart and transform my indifference and anger at my father into something else—empathy. A godly and wise friend of mine said that I should consider what my father went through when he was growing up and ask the Lord to give me a heart of compassion for him instead of anger. It took some time, but the Spirit began to change my posture toward my father to the point that over the course of several months, I crafted a letter of forgiveness to him.

After screening it through some friends, I was able to send that letter and let my father know that the slate was clean between us. Because I had been forgiven by God, I forgave him too. I also mentioned a few details in the letter about what he had been through growing up in a purposeful attempt to communicate empathy.

Now, if you had asked me several years ago what it would look like to show empathy towards my biological father, I probably would have said that you could have no idea what I'd been through, and I would have shut the conversation down. But gospel empathy had transformed my heart and made it not only possible to forgive but to extend and communicate empathy to a man who I'd been angry and indifferent toward for years and years.

So, where do we turn when it seems that anger and hate always win? We turn to Jesus because the gospel creates empathy in our hearts in a way that's seemingly impossible to imagine. What do we do when it's so easy to point the finger at other people and blame them for everything bad going on in the world? We remind ourselves of the undeserved salvation we've received and watch our anger transform into empathy by the power of God's Spirit. "For the Spirit God gave us does not make us timid, but gives us power, love and self-discipline" (2 Timothy 1:7). Jesus does the transforming because we are in him (2 Corinthians 5:17), and this is very good news.

People aren't our ultimate enemy. After all, Ephesians 6:12 says, "For our struggle is not against flesh and blood, but against the rulers, against the authorities, against the powers of this dark world and against the spiritual forces of evil in the heavenly realms." Understanding and embracing this drives us further up and further in to the gospel, and allows the Spirit to lead us to true heart change and empathy.

Empathy Creates Community

Empathy is the ability to understand and share the feelings of another, and a great character quality to have regardless of your relationship status with God. But gospel empathy takes this amazing character trait to a whole new level. It doesn't just treat the symptoms of bitterness and contempt in the human heart; it goes after the roots of the hatefulness and hostility in a way that literally nothing else can. My identity as a sinner saved by grace produces empathy for others because it shows me that I'm no better than anyone else—again, this is humility.

Although in his sinlessness he is superior to us in every way, Jesus is the ultimate example of humility because "he humbled himself by becoming obedient to death—even death on a cross!" (Philippians 2:8). Humility doesn't "one-up, one-down" everyone and keep looking to see who happens to be worse than me in whatever category. Humility rejects constant comparison, which makes it a key element in building empathy toward others—even others you strongly disagree with on certain issues.

And when true heart-level empathy is part of a person's character, there's a warmth to her or him that generates greater authentic connection with other people. My relationship with God strengthens me and provides me with what I need to love my enemies and extend empathy from the heart toward people who deserve the opposite, because that's exactly what Jesus did for me when he went to the cross.

Gospel empathy changes people from the heart outwards and attracts others to its beauty. Why? Because the gospel is always beautiful and always life-changing! There is nothing more attractive than a person who reflects the nature of their Savior, Jesus, and when people are drawn toward that kind of relational beauty, genuine community begins to flourish and nurture the detached soul.

Let me give you a few suggestions on how to practically foster gospel empathy, to functionally live as a fragrant aroma of Christ (2 Corinthians 2:14-15), and to move toward unity instead of isolation:

1. Ask good questions of the people you disagree with in a desire to understand their viewpoint and love them in the way God does

When you see opposing sides squabble with one another, questions are often used as ammunition against the other side as opposed to displaying a sincere desire to seek a greater understanding of what an opponent thinks and feels. But what if we asked heartfelt questions of the people we disagreed with in a genuine attempt to understand why they think and feel the way they do? What if our goal was to figure out the heart behind their arguments in an attempt to empathize and connect instead of demonize and destroy? Having a genuine curiosity and legitimately listening to someone's answers can really help you gain Christ-like empathy for others and grow in affection for them as fellow human beings made in God's image. In my life, I've found that people usually feel cared for and loved when they feel listened to, so asking good questions of the people you might consider your "enemy" on a certain topic might be a fantastic way to love them in the way Jesus calls us to love in Matthew 5:43-48.

2. Break out of your comfort zone every now and then and put yourself in new environments

Along a similar line, it can be good to physically move to arenas where you know you'll be uncomfortable. Have you ever attended an atheist meeting? Ever gone to a political event where you know you'll disagree with the things that will be celebrated there? Have you ever been invited to a party that you know is going to be an alcohol-soaked night of chaos—and then showed up and lived differently? Now, you might be thinking, "I'd never set foot in a place like that." But let me encourage you to consider seeking the discomfort of moving into spaces that you'd ordinarily feel uneasy about approaching. If you push yourself to move away from your comfort zone every now and then and visit places you'd not normally frequent, you'll find that it humanizes the people you have a natural tendency to stereotype. It even gives you the opportunity to ask the questions we were just talking about, but to do so on their turf.

It can be easier to invite people to come to your Bible study, your campus ministry, your church, or your youth group (and that's great—keep doing that!), but a lot of our friends who don't know Christ will never move toward an environment that they associate with God or Christianity in general. There could be a variety of reasons why someone might never darken the doorway of a Christian event, so why not put the discomfort on yourself and meet them where they feel most at home or comfortable? If you do, you may be surprised by how much they appreciate you showing up, and you might start to see God move in your heart with gospel empathy at the same time. Showing care by showing up and moving toward people instead of demonizing them will mold and shape you into the kind of person God will use to bring others to Jesus. And when an enemy becomes a sibling in Christ, there is no greater example of how the gospel creates community among seemingly polar-opposite individuals.

3. Make a list of the people who make you most angry and pray for their well-being

In Luke 6:27-28, Jesus says, "Love your enemies, do good to those who hate you, bless those who curse you, pray for those who mistreat you." Um, I don't know about you, but I think this one's tough. This is one of those commandments from Jesus that I prickle at when I read it. However, as a Christ-follower, I need to hear it and be reminded to adopt this posture over and over again. It's somewhat easy to pray for the people who make you happy or comfortable—but loving, doing good to, blessing, and praying for the people who consistently bother me or make me mad? Yikes. It's a good thing that God has put his Spirit inside of us as believers (Romans 8:9; 2 Corinthians 1:22) and given us the ability through him to do the seemingly impossible.

While it may feel like a huge obstacle to overcome, I'd really encourage you to grab your phone and list out the people in your life who upset you, anger you, bother you, or regularly annoy you. Then, in a spirit of obedience, by the power of the Holy Spirit, pray for every one of your "enemies" by name and ask God to bless them. Again, this might seem completely insurmountable to you at first, but you'll be surprised by how, over time, prayer can soften your heart toward the people you dislike. And as the softening process happens (again, this may take a while), gospel empathy can form in ways you previously believed would never happen. An effective antidote to anger and polarization is habitual prayer for the people you struggle with the most.

Okay, deep breath. I know that was a lot, but why don't you take a moment right now and ask God to personally go after the roots of your heart? Ask him to help you form gospel empathy for the people you might consider to be on the "other side" of your convictions and opinions about any given topic. Ask him to mold and shape you more into the image of Christ and, if you don't have it already, to generate a heart of empathy in you that hasn't been present before. Ask him to transform your anger and any hatred into an empathy that will create harmonious community. Only Christ, through the power of the Holy Spirit who lives in you, can make genuine and lasting change.

The fruit of angry polarization is isolation and pain. But gospel empathy flips the script on our selfish hearts in a way that is impossible for us to manufacture on our own through sheer will power to "be better." Our call is to cry out to God and ask him to be gracious to us, that we might form the kind of community our lonely hearts long for—community centered around Jesus, which actually practices the kind of gospel empathy we've been talking about.

To his own discomfort, Christ moved toward us, so let's die to our own self ambition, take up our cross, and follow him by moving toward others with gospel empathy.

Reflection Questions

1. How have you experienced polarization and anger toward "the other side," and how have those postures injured you and your relationships (or the relationships of people around you)?
2. Can you think of an example or two of how you've seen the gospel extinguish the fires of

anger? How have you seen anger transform into empathy by the power of the Spirit?

3. How have you seen God at work producing gospel empathy in you? If you haven't seen a real heart-level change in your life, ask God right now to tackle the roots of your sin and create in you a heart of gospel empathy that fosters union with others instead of anger and isolation. Read Psalm 51 and cry out for mercy from God. Ask him to wash you, forgive you, and change you into someone new, who sees Spirit-driven empathy create genuine community.

PART FOUR:

Emotion

CHAPTER 7

Deepening the Disconnect: Depression and Anxiety

"I feel like God messed up when he made me. I don't really have a sense of purpose or worth, and I'm just sad all the time."

That's what Jack said to his small-group Bible study one evening in the middle of the second year after graduating from college. He had been struggling with depression off and on since early high school, but now it seemed that this dark cloud of looming despair consistently hung over him, and it wouldn't go away. What he was feeling was significantly different and worse than in the past, and it made him want to retreat to the comfort and safety of his apartment literally all of the time.

In the process of getting ready to grab dinner before the campus ministry large-group meeting, Amber felt a tightness in her chest unlike anything she'd experienced before. Her heart was racing, her hands were trembling, and sweat was gathering on her forehead. She'd been thinking about the large crowd and about trying to make conversation with a bunch of other students for the night, but now it felt as if there might be something horribly wrong with her. After visiting the on-campus medical-emergency building, Amber was told by a doctor that she wasn't dying but had experienced a full-blown panic attack. After that experience, Amber struggled to leave her dorm room, which felt like the only safe, comfortable environment she could control.

Jack's and Amber's stories are not unfamiliar. It seems as if nearly everyone is only one degree of separation away from another person who has wrestled with depression and/or anxiety at some point. Or maybe you have gone through something like this or are going through it right now.

If so, I just want to say how sorry I am that you're experiencing something so difficult and, at times, debilitating. Someone very close to me has struggled with depression and anxiety, and I've seen how heavy and dark it can be; it's awful.

I also want to note that mental health struggles are a different kind of hurt that contributes to a sense of loneliness and isolation. Things like depression and anxiety can catch you off guard and create loneliness (or stem from loneliness) and are deeply painful. It's a different kind of trap than digital identity, porn, casual sex, tribalism or anger. But because depression and anxiety are more than prevalent in our culture right now, I wanted to make sure I talked about their relevance to the loneliness in our lives.

Depression, Anxiety, and Loneliness

When it comes to young people's mental well-being, the Healthy Minds Study[19] found that 44% of college students reported symptoms of depression, 37% reported anxiety disorders, and 15% reported having seriously considered suicide in the past year. These are the highest recorded rates in the history of the 15-year-old study.[20] But as depression and anxiety have continually risen over the last several years among young people, loneliness has tagged right along with them. In a recent survey, the Newport Institute found that chronic loneliness in young adults is associated with a reduced sense of meaning and purpose—a symptom closely linked to depression and anxiety.[21] It also found that being lonely creates a 33% higher chance of depression and a 16-fold increase in the risk of death by suicide.[22]

It seems that when the haze of depression clouds all of life, the social connections a person needs often suffer. There are, of course, several reasons why this can happen, but being in college ministry has given me a front row seat to a few major ones. Most notably, depression and anxiety can make a person go inward and focus solely on themselves, often to the neglect of much needed community. They regularly prevent people from reaching out to others and engaging in social activities.[23]

In this state of mind, it's difficult to believe that anyone else understands what you're going through, so turning inward is a natural reaction, especially in our Western culture, where individualism is valued above almost everything or anyone else. The "you are enough" posters and yard signs confirm that it all rides on my ability to fix myself without anyone's help. "I got this," we silently remind ourselves over again to the detriment of authentic connections with other people who can and want to care, listen, love, and help us when we desperately need it.

The default and strong temptation is simply to go it alone.

Alone Versus Lonely

I want to be clear that I'm not just talking about isolation here. There are plenty of people who can be on their own but not feel a shred of loneliness. Conversely, there are people who spend lots of time with other people and yet can still feel desperately lonely. Being alone isn't the same thing as being lonely. So, getting on the solution side of our epidemic of loneliness isn't as simple as just being around people more often.

But even while we wrestle with depression and anxiety, as we saw in the first section, the evidence for the desire to be in genuine community with others still exists, though it's displayed mostly digitally via things like social media or interactive online video games. There's assumed social safety behind the digital shield of a phone, laptop, or video game console, but we know that connection with others through pixels won't ever truly provide the antidote to the loneliness that's frequently coupled with depression and anxiety.

Quarantining yourself from the world and digitally plugging in when mental health issues begin to flare up is the opposite of the solution. Detachment from others when life hurts makes the hurt much worse. If you're longing for a digital connection even when you're alone, it's a big flashing arrow that points you to the realization that you don't just need to be around others, but that you have a need to be known too. When we're struggling mentally, we still need to be challenged by others, encouraged by others, and held accountable by others. This is what we should be praying for and actively seeking: purposeful, godly involvement from others who care enough about you to point you in the right direction—but also throw their arm around you and help you fight the good fight of faith when all you can do is slowly limp forward.

Hebrews 10:24-25 says, "And let us consider how we may spur one another on toward love and good deeds, not giving up meeting together, as some are in the habit of doing, but encouraging one another—and all the more as you see the Day approaching." Face-to-face interactions with other people are what the

Scriptures call us toward, so showing up to events, Bible studies, one-on-one discipleship times, worship sessions, teaching times, church services, and any other gatherings with brothers and sisters in Christ is incredibly important to keep our heads above water.

Humility says, "I haven't got this. I need help." God gives grace to the humble (1 Peter 5:5, ESV), often via other Christ-following people who can come alongside you and be part of the solution in your battles with anxiety and depression. Everything you're dealing with doesn't have to rest on your shoulders alone. The first step, before we get into the meat of the next chapter, is to admit your need and ask someone you trust to engage with you and help you.

Reflection Questions

1. What has been your personal experience with depression and anxiety? How have you seen those mental health issues impact your life and the lives of others around you in negative ways?
2. Have you tried to "fix yourself" when these issues arise? Why do you think that greater self-reliance might lead directly to greater loneliness in life?
3. What do you think it would practically look like for you to know and be known by others in a godly community that spurred one another on toward love and good deeds?

CHAPTER 8

Authentic Healing: Gospel Involvement

"Living as if we are independent beings, free to live on our own and do our own thing, will never work."[24]

Paul David Tripp

It's always a little tricky to talk about mental health issues in our current culture. It seems as if anyone at anytime can step on a proverbial land mine and upset someone else if they try to address the subject with nuance. This isn't a mental health book, and I'm not a mental health expert, but I want to offer you some practical suggestions from my experience that I believe will be helpful for you when you're ready to try them.

But before we dive into this chapter, I think it's important to remind you about who you are in Christ and the unique perspective we should have on this subject as followers of Jesus.

God the Holy Spirit lives inside of you as a Christian, and he gives you the power to live the life of a believer. Consequently, we have resources available to us as Christians that others do not have. As you proactively depend on the Spirit to live the Christian life in and through you, you're able to experience becoming more and more like Jesus as you surrender to his power and control. (Theologians call this "sanctification.") Yes, you may still struggle with things like poor mental health, anxiety or depression, but because you are a believer, you have the best dad anyone could ever dream of, wrapping his loving arms around you in tender care and compassion as you struggle with life's problems and trials. It's vital to keep that truth at the forefront of your mind and heart as we talk about depression and anxiety.

Next, the Bible itself gives practical wisdom that aligns with science about what's healthy for the brain. Meditation on Scripture (Psalm 1:2), practicing God's presence (16:8), living with gratitude (1 Thessalonians 5:18), encouraging others intentionally and daily (Hebrews 3:13), living generously (2 Corinthians 9:6-7), and serving others (Mark 10:43-45) are all practices that science suggests can bring well-being to our brains and help us engage intentionally with other people in healthier (and holier) ways.

Because we have a new identity in Christ, things shift rather significantly when we know that we don't wrestle with and fight mental health problems "like a boxer beating the air" (1 Corinthians 9:26). Our battle is never futile because the presence of God in our lives gives us purpose. Not only do we have the assurance that God the Holy Spirit lives inside of us as our every-moment companion, but we can also experience the presence of God through his people. Involvement in a church community of gospel-focused followers of Jesus helps us see the hands and feet of Christ walking alongside us in our struggles against the heavy weights of anxiety and depression.

Autonomous Bondage

Many in our culture assume the opposite of what we've been highlighting so far. They assume that safety requires freedom from others: freedom from commitment and something as close to full autonomy as possible. When others get involved in our lives, things can feel messy and, for some, unsafe. Consequently, plenty of people opt for comfort over complexity, so they isolate in an attempt to find protection from additional harm. But frighteningly enough, that freedom regularly leaves people enslaved to an untethered empty self.[25] If autonomy is the goal in life instead of submission to Christ's authority, a person is actually in bondage to autonomy itself.

John 8:36 says, "So if the Son sets you free, you will be free indeed." See, a lot of people think that Christianity is a religion that comes along and tells me what I'm not allowed to do anymore. It draws confining and claustrophobic boundary lines around my life, choking out all the fun, excitement, pleasure, and freedom I desire and want to experience. It prevents me from enjoying the freedom and autonomy I think I need and want. But a relationship with God through Jesus Christ isn't about restrictions. It's actually about freedom from the existing restrictions already in your life that you don't even know are there. Galatians 5:1 says, "It is for freedom that Christ has set us free. Stand firm, then, and do not let yourselves be burdened again by a yoke of slavery." Christianity isn't about slavery to a set of rules—it's about emancipation from the slavery you're already in and can't even see.

Jesus isn't about locking you into a lifestyle of behavior change. Ick. He's about releasing you as a prisoner from the jail cell of the independence we all naturally worship and are unknowingly imprisoned by. (How's that for a mind-bender?) The quest for autonomy in life—to seek whatever it is that satisfies our ambitions and comforts—is a "me-focused" way to live, and when life doesn't manifest in the way we'd like, it becomes this ever illusive mirage on the horizon that we keep chasing but can never grasp.

Now, I'm not saying if you're depressed or anxious that you're a self-focused person, but I know that when I'm in pain of any kind, it can be easy to shut everyone else out in the belief that, "Nobody understands what I'm going through, so I'm not going to even try to explain it anymore." But as already mentioned, isolation leads directly to loneliness, and the vicious circle of increasing mental health problems continues.

Jesus, however, loves you enough to keep "pestering" you and wooing you back to him and his family of believers. He wants to give you a gospel purpose that's bigger than yourself. Self-focused people are the most miserable people in the world—and Jesus knows this. He's calling us to draw our focus up to him. He wants us to put our lives into his care because he's the most capable being in the universe. There is literally no one more trustworthy to hand our lives over to than the one who loves us and gave himself up for us.

And if the Son has set you free, you will be free indeed.

One Burning Coal

Dwight L. Moody was an American evangelist and publisher who lived in the 1800s. The story has been told that Moody was visiting a prominent Chicago citizen when the idea of church membership and involvement came up in their conversation.

"I believe I can be just as good a Christian outside the church without involvement as I can be inside it with involvement," the man said.

Moody said nothing. Instead, he moved to the fireplace, where a fire was blazing against the winter outside; he removed one burning coal and placed it on the hearth. The two men sat together and watched the ember die out.

"I see," the other man said.[26]

I know it can be super easy to think that we have to fix our own problems, especially if we've been hurt by others before or are struggling with shame of some kind. But in seclusion is where the enemy wants to keep you. When it's hunting, a lion doesn't excuse itself passing through a herd of antelope and pick out its favorite from the middle of the pack to eat. No, it looks for the straggler on the outskirts that's alone and vulnerable by itself. The Bible says that Satan prowls around like a roaring lion looking for someone to devour (1 Peter 5:8), so when the pain of mental health problems pushes us to detach from others, it's crucial that we ask God to help us push back and move toward involvement in gospel-rich community. In the war with mental health problems, you will always be stronger in the company of other Christians who care about you.

As much as someone might think they can keep going and keep growing with just this "me and Jesus" perspective, the truth is that the deep connection and spiritual flourishing we all crave often happens downstream from intentional commitment to a local church. In reality, you can't go it alone—the Bible doesn't give you that option if you're a believer. Jesus comes for his stray sheep; he seeks us out and invites us into the family even when we're hurting. He is the one who has the power to connect us with other believers as we take steps of faith to reach out, let others in on our struggles, and invite them to be actively involved in our lives. Jesus is your help, my friend. You don't need to pull yourself up by your bootstraps to get better. He can help you do the things needed in your life to move towards health and vibrancy. I know that can feel impossible under the weight of anxiety and/or depression, but nothing is impossible with God (Luke 1:37, ESV).

As Christ helps you get healthy, he regularly does that through the avenue of the family of God. Why? Because we're called to be actively involved in one another's lives, laughing and crying together in all the beautiful ups and catastrophic downs. "Rejoice with those who rejoice; mourn with those who mourn," says Romans 12:15.

"Carry each other's burdens," Scripture also says, "and in this way you will fulfill the law of Christ" (Galatians 6:2). As we saw in chapter 2, if you love Jesus, you're a vital part of the body of Christ, working in tandem with other believers, who care about you while you care about them. Letting others in doesn't make you a burden to your friends—it gives your friends the opportunity to be an instrument in God's hands to nurture and help you when you need it the most!

One Christian woman who shared her battle with depression said it felt as if she was trudging through peanut butter trying to do anything. However, she was taking proactive steps to get involved in a women's Bible study, accept invitations for dinner out with friends, and share life with other believers whenever possible. And in taking the initiative to fold herself into community with fellow Christians, she said it felt as if Jesus was throwing her a life preserver (lifebuoy) of grace. It was a reminder that she was not a burden to her friends and family, and that there is joy, hope, and grace to be found by letting others in.

This story might sound overwhelming to you if you're struggling right now, because stepping out may seem like too big a leap. If that's you, let me reassure you that taking tiny steps to connect with community is okay! Sometimes we just need to take things day by day, if not hour by hour, when life is completely overwhelming. There's no shame in slow progress.

Commitment

Commitment to the work of the gospel alongside others in a church community proactively helps us to fight against the struggles we come face to face with in everyday life. When we're overwhelmed with the battle, the answer isn't less involvement in the things of God ("I'm tired, and I need a break"); it's actually more involvement in gospel-related things ("I'm exhausted, and I need to take the focus off myself and get involved alongside others as I wrestle with this").

Now, that doesn't mean it's not appropriate to take a breather every now and then and say no to certain things if you're on the verge of burnout. If you need some time off, it's certainly okay to take some. However, something I've found is that many young people have retreated from involvement in the name of fear more than in the name of taking a healthy break.

Everything you do in life is an overflow of your heart, so it's important to protect and nurture it (Proverbs 4:23), but sometimes your heart needs to be preached to and exhorted to move into the potential discomfort of involving others in your life. So ask yourself when you feel the dissonance, "Would it be unwise for me to commit to move into community right now, or am

I uncomfortable because I'm feeling fearful, lazy, or apathetic? Do I need to push through this discomfort to engage with other believers because it's what God is calling me to do?" Finding the heart-level answers to those questions is vital, so be honest with yourself about your motivation (or lack of motivation) for getting involved.

Weirdly enough, in my many years of ministry, I have seen over and over again that our souls can actually find healthy rest when we are more involved in a church community, not less. When we have the ability and intention to focus on others and not just ourselves, we're living in a Christ-like way, which satisfies our hearts with a sense of purpose since serving is what we have been made for (Mark 10:43-45). And when we exercise with serving hearts instead of self-focused hearts (all within the context of godly community), there's a rest that can only be experienced on the other side of the service exercise itself.

Sure, sometimes restraint is needed when it comes to more involvement with Christian community—but sometimes discipline needs to be implemented instead. Only you know your heart motivation for getting involved in a gospel-focused church community. I'm simply asking you to question what's actually going on in your heart, because serving others in godly companionship is such a strategic way to fight loneliness and mental health issues.

Soul-nourishing Bible studies, the excitement of sharing your faith, heartfelt community prayer, serving the needy, and caring discipleship are all intentional disciplines that kick against anxiety, depression, and loneliness triggers. The temptation is always to do less when the negative feelings come, but your inclination to separate from other committed believers should be fought with vigor. The spiritual nourishment we can help provide because of our commitment to Christ and one another is priceless. And when times get tough (not if, but when), we'll have each other's backs when we need to be spiritually propped up.

Commitment is a word that some avoid using because of the baggage that can often be associated with it. Phrases like "tied down," "trapped," or "held back" are often linked to commitment, and that doesn't mesh well with expressive individualism. But commitment, when observed through a healthy connection to other Christ-followers, is not just a good thing but a great thing.

Take friendship for example. Listen to these words from John 15:14-15: "You are my friends if you do what I command. I no longer call you servants, because a servant does not know his master's business. Instead, I have called you friends, for everything that I learned from my Father I have made known to you." If you are in Christ, you have friendship with God, and, like any friend, he desires fellowship with you.[27] God is the ultimate reliable friend, who, you can be sure, isn't going anywhere. He's committed to you—he's so committed that he gave his only Son for you. Christian friends are to mirror the beauty of commitment as they have experienced it with God to one another. Committed friendship ushers in health, acceptance, and security—the very opposite of being trapped.

Committed friendship looks like keeping plans when you make them instead of cancelling at the last minute because something better comes along. It looks like being a safe person for your friend to share vulnerable details of their life with in confidence, which won't be told to anyone else. It looks like mutual accountability, answering 3 a.m. phone calls when you're needed, purposeful reminders about who you are in Christ, and meme-riddled, hilarious text threads. Committed friendship is delightful reliability, not bleak obligation.

And this is only one way of flipping the negative connotation on its head. In fact, I'd argue that the troubles that can regularly come with things like depression, loneliness, and anxiety are often diminished (or at least made bearable) because of the way God uses committed friends in our lives. Commitment, in reality, is a phenomenal thing.

When we stand alongside our committed friends within a committed body of believers who stick around even when things get extra challenging, we're a part of something greater than our individual selves. We find spiritual brothers, sisters, mothers, and fathers. We find generation gaps and people who are totally different from us—but we're all united together by our love for Jesus. We're folded into a gospel culture that says, "Yes and welcome" to us because we share in the identity that's above any other potential identity. We share the identity of being a child of God—an immediate member of God's family.

When we are involved in the work of the church, meaning replaces isolation. Unity replaces loneliness. Community replaces individualism. Family replaces detachment.

If depression and anxiety frequently carry loneliness into your life, commitment to a local gospel-focused church family carries companionship. Gospel involvement looks like serving others with their tangible needs and giving of yourself so that others would benefit. It looks like studying the Bible among a group of people who dive deep into the living and active word of God. It looks like accountability and challenge, friendship and laughter, mission and purpose, spiritual growth and maturity. It looks like putting your hand on a hurting person's shoulder and saying, "Let's pray."

Moving Towards Thriving

Everything that loneliness isn't can be found by getting involved in a gospel community that cares about following Jesus and his word. If you want to thrive in community instead of flounder in isolation, here are some practical steps:

1. Find a Bible-believing church and get involved to become part of the solution in its mission

Not only will you find yourself connected to genuine followers of Christ, but you'll be used by the Lord in ways that proactively care for others while deepening your relationship with God. Becoming an often-used instrument in the hands of our Father is a gracious act of God to inject purpose into our lives. It's a life-enriching catalyst that overshadows much of what causes depression, anxiety, and loneliness for us. God chooses to use us to help others, and when we obediently live in submission to his plans for us, we become all the more connected to him, his heart, and his people.

2. Bond with others together in the context of ministry

Some of the greatest examples of when I've felt the most connection and camaraderie in gospel community was when I was shoulder to shoulder with fellow believers doing ministry together. In fact, I'd venture to say that everyone who's ever been a super close friend of mine was someone who I was in ministry with at one point in time. When you study God's word together, go on a mission trip together, pour into people in discipleship together, share the gospel together, or do anything else that's ministry related together, you're doing more than just an activity alongside another person—you're bonding as you battle together! There's both a spoken and unspoken unification that happens with fellow believers in Christ when you fight the good fight alongside them as brothers and sisters—and you naturally bond with the people you're in battle with (1 Timothy 6:12).

Many of my greatest relational memories are ones that formed in the spiritual trenches with people who loved Jesus, loved me, and loved being involved in gospel work next to me. I can't speak for everyone of course, but my times of greatest emotional and mental health have been in the context of ministry alongside other believers as we walk in the same direction of obedience to Christ.

3. If you're suffering from depression or persistent, dark anxiousness coupled with panic, it's a good thing to see a doctor

Now, I know this specific topic can be quite controversial, but I believe that God works through advancements in modern medicine. I suffer from chronic migraines, and my doctor has really helped me by prescribing a specific kind of medicine to combat and eliminate those migraines when they hit me. I thank the Lord for how it has made it possible for me to go on with my day without pain after a migraine headache strikes. I'd be miserable without that medicine. Similarly, if depression and oppressive anxious thoughts or feelings are deeply impacting your life, I think you should get on the solution side of that by pursuing both counseling and physiological options to combat what's hurting you.

I'm not saying that medicine is the best solution for everyone who suffers from depression and/or anxiety, but I've seen the Lord use technological advancements in science, psychology, engineering, medicine, and a whole lot of other areas to bring care and peace when someone is suffering. Consequently, I think it's wise to pursue medical solutions as a part of exploring ways to get healthy if a trusted doctor believes it will help you. If medicine can help alleviate what's assaulting you (without a bunch of horrible side effects), then I think you should look into it.

Also, don't be ashamed to ask around and see what has helped some of your friends or family—you won't be alone in seeking medical options to mitigate oppressive mental health struggles. The body of Christ can and will be part of the resolution in this area of your life if you don't try to handle it in seclusion.

Yes, Jesus will love you just the same if you never move toward more gospel involvement. But I really believe that you will miss out on many of the greatest aspects of abundant life if you remain in isolation as a Christian: being known and loved, knowing and loving others, receiving and giving grace and truth, experiencing joy and strength when you least expect it, and having others pray over you when it's too heavy to pray for yourself. And that's just scratching the surface of what God can provide for you through his body of believers.

Have you ever seen a group of people doing something super fun like a game or activity, and then one person in the group pauses, turns to look at you, and says, "You gotta get in on this!"? Well, involvement in gospel community is the best activity out there, and it's as if Jesus himself is pausing, looking at you, and saying, "Hey, my friend, you gotta get in on this!"

Gospel involvement is participation in something much bigger than ourselves. And when we draw our focus up to our magnificent Savior, away from the circumstances and issues in our own lives, we're able to experience him folding us into the kind of community that can truly bring authentic healing to our anxious and depressed hearts.

Reflection Questions

1. Why do you think commitment to a body of believers is so vital for your personal walk with God? In the past, how have you seen God use fellow believers in your life to grow you and help you to change the lives of other people around you?
2. Why do you think self-focused people are often the most miserable people in the world? Think of an example of when you acted selfishly and how it made you more miserable instead of happy and content.
3. If everything we do in life is an overflow of our hearts, does your heart currently need to be protected, or does your heart need to be challenged to engage when it comes to your personal involvement in a gospel community?

CONCLUSION

The Long Game

"A man reaps what he sows."

Galatians 6:7b

I remember being on the military base right before my senior year of high school and hugging my mom, dad, and sister to say one final goodbye before they moved to Central America. I was staying behind to live with a different family so I could graduate in the States and not have to go to a fourth high school in four years.

I was so sad and thoroughly confused as to why God would allow this to happen in my life. In the car driving away from my family, I felt so lonely. Nobody understood what I was going through. Nobody knew my pain. Nobody comprehended how isolating it was to be a military kid with this many moves under his belt as a 17-year-old. I hated it, and I didn't see how God could bring anything good out of it.

But then, over the course of my final year of high school, being away from my family forced me to step out of my social comfort zone and engage with friends, my foster family, the teachers at my school, and my fellow long-distance runners on the cross country team, in ways I never would have if my family had been there as normal. That year ended up (in many ways) shaping me into who I am today. The social skills I now have are because of that difficult year. I'm now able to strike up a conversation with almost anyone because that year taught me how to really engage in community and grow into a more socially capable person. The loneliness I initially felt when my family moved away molded me in positive ways, which I still utilize today, decades later.

The times when I have felt most alone in life are the times when God has met me in the most profound ways. The hard part is actually pushing through the loneliness and entering into the work God wants me to engage in so I can then experience genuine healing and true connection with him and with others. The gospel can heal our epidemic of loneliness, and the healing process itself is something God can and will utilize to make us more like Jesus if we choose to invest in relationship with him and rely on our Christian brothers and sisters.

We will all reap what we sow (Galatians 6:7), and it's important to look at our lives and ask honestly, "What kinds of seeds am I currently sowing?"

If loneliness is prevalent in your life and you hate it, the easiest temptation might be to try to find life and connection in the faulty crutches we've explored in this book or in a million other things to make the pain of isolation go away. There could be countless reasons for why you might be experiencing loneliness. At one time or other, all of us feel like the psalmist King David, who cried out to God, "Turn to me and be gracious to me, for I am lonely and afflicted" (Psalm 25:16).

Hope for the Hopeless

Before he died, the *Friends* actor Matthew Perry wrote in his memoir, "I am constantly filled with a lurking loneliness, a yearning, clinging to the notion that something outside of me will fix me. But I had had all that the outside had to offer!"[28]

Matthew Perry had everything the world could present to him, but he still felt lonely. Now, you might read a quote like that from a famous actor and think, "What hope is there for anyone if even people like him are experiencing the crushing effects of loneliness? It's useless!"

Well, first, sadly in this case, he didn't know the love of God in Jesus. But second, if you can't imagine getting to a place where loneliness is behind you, it's important to remember that the battle is usually a long game instead of a short one. In my senior year of high school, it took a while not only to get through the loneliness but also to figure out how God used that difficult and painful situation to bring about lifelong positive change in me. Those seeds that were sown took a while to blossom, but they did eventually bloom in my life—and I'm overwhelmingly grateful to God for the fact that they did.

Some Practicals

Once again, I'm about to get super practical. As we wrap this book up, allow me to give you a few final ways to fight loneliness and grab the opportunities God presents to you so you can grow closer to him and others.

1. If you haven't already, submit your life to Christ and tell him that he calls the shots from here on out

Yes, Jesus is your Savior (1 John 4:14), but he is also your Lord (John 20:28), meaning he's the one who is master and commander of where your life goes. If you only want Jesus to be your Savior but not your Lord—sorry, but he doesn't give you that option. (Read about the cost of being a disciple in Luke 14:25-35.) It's a package deal when someone admits and believes the truth of the gospel, because you can't take one without the other (Savior AND Lord). When your life is under the lordship of Jesus, he may take you to places where you are hesitant to go, but that will always be for the purpose of producing something in you that you'd never be able to manufacture on your own.[29] Submit to his authority in your life because, when you do, you'll grow closer to him and to the other women and men who have chosen to submit as well—those people in the family of God will be some of the best friends you'll ever have.

2. Remember that you're never really alone

Jesus said in Matthew 28:20, "And surely I am with you always..." meaning that he'll never abandon you. So even though you may feel in those isolating moments as if nobody cares about, loves, or understands you—it simply isn't true. Jesus is the great Shepherd; he always gets it (he faced an abundance of isolation himself), and he's always close. In fact, the apostle Paul says in Acts 17:27 that God is "not far from any one of us," and at the time, Paul was speaking to a group of Greek idol-worshipers, who didn't even know the real God. How much more, because of Jesus, are we able to rest assured that God is always near, always present, always by our side guiding us? We may feel lonely sometimes (or even a lot), but we need to take God at his word and trust that he's not far—ever. Author, speaker, and poet Jackie Hill Perry once said, "God asks us to trust him even when it doesn't line up with how we feel."[30] So when you feel the absence of much-needed community and companionship, remind yourself that you're never truly alone. The Creator of all things is close to you.

3. Invest in a small group of people and go deep with them

We've touched on this already, but I think it's worth revisiting again. As well as my wife, there are a few friends in my life with whom I am intentionally vulnerable and like to meet with as frequently as possible.

One is my friend Brian, who lives in a different state. Even though Brian and I don't see each other in person very often, we purposefully do a video call once a month for at least an hour and a half each time to talk about our lives, joke around, share hardships, and pray for each other. Yes, he lives hours away from me, but I feel super connected to him because we're intentional about talking each month. The other main person I connect with is Gabe. He's a local friend who works at my home church as the youth pastor. Gabe and I text pretty much every day, we see each other casually at church events, and we also schedule an every-other-week time together to grab lunch and talk about anything and everything. My times with him have been some of the most gospel-rich, honest, vulnerable, and hilarious times of my life. It isn't an exaggeration to say that these friends have been two highlights of my life over the last five years. God has used them in amazing ways to connect with me and foster a deep sense of community in my life that I'm eternally grateful for.

But five years ago, I didn't really have any of those kinds of friends to share life with, and it was incredibly lonely. Even though I had (and still have!) a wife and kids, I needed deep friendships with men like Brian and Gabe to see and experience life with too. I had to put myself out there and ask if they were willing to meet with consistency and vulnerability (and that was kind of scary), but I did it with both Brian and Gabe, and God has richly blessed me as a result. It doesn't have to be more than a few people, but pray and ask God to provide you with the kind of friends you need to walk alongside with God. Lean into the discomfort of it—when you allow yourself to be vulnerable, you'll find you are continuously thankful that God has blessed you with those deep friendships.

4. Love others without expectation

In other words, connect with people in a non-transactional way. This may sound a bit odd at first, but as you interact with people around you every day, try to avoid thinking of them as vending machines. Let me explain what I mean: whether you realize it or not, you're probably sizing up everyone you interact with in a way that analyzes whether they are beneficial to you or not. "What can they do for me?" is the default question our brains ask, even though it may never come out of our mouths or fully form in our consciousness. That might seem irreverent to you, but if you take a moment to pause and evaluate how you treat people and why you treat them the way you do, you'll quickly come to the realization that you're likely looking at others through the lens of transactions most of the time.

This guy gives you your coffee. That girl you talked to makes you feel desirable. That guy said or did something funny that made you laugh. This girl commiserated with you about how bad the football game was last weekend and validated your frustration with the team. That guy could probably connect you with the right person so you can land that internship. Do you see the pattern in these examples? Each person gives you something worth your interaction with him or her: coffee, an ego-stroke, laughter, validation, or personal benefits like an internship.

Now, those things in and of themselves aren't bad, but what if we gave people our time and attention and didn't expect anything in return? What if we put in the dollar bills of attentiveness and kindness toward others but never expected the reward we "paid for" with our time, attention, and care to drop at the bottom of the vending machine afterwards? What if we didn't do to get but just loved others without expecting anything back from them? Here's what would happen—you'd more than likely be a lot less miserable and lonely.

When we don't expect anything in return from people as we joyfully give them our time, attention, money, etc., we aren't disappointed as much. We aren't offended as much. We aren't as annoyed as we used to be. We don't complain about how people don't live up to our expectations. We connect with people (in both short and long interactions) simply to connect with people and reflect the goodness of God to them. This way of living helps to inject your life with purpose, adventure, community, hospitality, and action. When you look to give instead of get, there aren't ulterior motives in your giving—which puts you very much in line with the ultimate life-giving spirit himself, Jesus Christ (1 Corinthians 15:45). Speaking of which...

5. Model your life after the way Jesus described himself in Mark 10:45

When Jesus was unpacking the upside-down principles of God's kingdom to his disciples, he capped off a teaching with this self-description: "For even the Son of Man did not come to be served, but to serve, and to give his life as a ransom for many" (Mark 10:45). At the risk of over-simplifying the Christian life, this verse essentially defines what it means to be a disciple of Jesus. The culture around us and our sinful nature communicate, "Your life for mine." In other words, "If I can get ahead by you falling behind, sign me up." Christianity, however, says just the opposite: "My life for yours." Putting others first and dying to yourself is the bread and butter of what it means to follow Christ, and much like the refusal to treat people transactionally, dying to yourself and living as a servant is how Jesus would have us go about our daily lives—because that's exactly how he went about his everyday life. And when you align yourself with the way Christ lived, you share in his sufferings and commune with him in ways that draw you closer to God.

I'm reminded here of Jesus' words in Matthew 16:24-25, when he says, "Whoever wants to be my disciple must deny themselves and take up their cross and follow me. For whoever wants to save their life will lose it, but whoever loses their life for me will find it." It's interesting to imagine what his disciples must have been thinking when he said this to them. We're reading from the perspective of people who know what Jesus did by dying on the cross, but his disciples didn't know this at the time. They must have been thinking, *Take up your cross? Roman execution? Why would Jesus tell us to die by Roman execution and then follow him afterward? That doesn't make any sense—I don't get it!* But they inevitably did get it when Jesus led the way by doing the exact thing he had asked his followers to do.

Christ will never ask you to go anywhere he hasn't first already gone. He wouldn't ask you to die without first dying himself. He doesn't ask you to sacrifice anything he hasn't already given up. Yes, Jesus asks a lot of his followers, but he's already done the work and embodied a life of selflessness. And when we, by the power of the Holy Spirit, live a life of selflessness and servanthood the way Christ did (as his Spirit lives in us, brings about change, and gives us help and strength), we connect more deeply not only with his heart but with the hearts of other disciples who take up their cross daily and follow him. There's no community like the community of others who make it their life's focus to live like the Savior. So seek out those who live as if their life belongs not to them but to the one who bought it at a price (1 Corinthians 6:19-20).

These are just a few practical ways to apply what we've been talking about since page 1 of this book. Again—it's a long game, not a short one. Relationships take time to build, so be patient as you look to connect with other people.

Additionally, the process of being refined by God is generally something that happens over a long period of time too. So, as you're being sanctified and growing to be more and more like Jesus, you'll discover with greater clarity how the gospel can heal our epidemic of loneliness. Like a small acorn that grows into a mighty tree, it's a process that requires patience and time. Rarely will your loneliness be alleviated overnight.

Life is often characterized by the 10,000 little moments you live every day[31] that all add up to the sum of who you've become, so don't be discouraged that you can't life-hack your way into close and fulfilling connections with others. It takes work, intentionality, endurance, and prayer. Remember that what you've sown you will reap (Galatians 6:7), so in those 10,000 little moments today, invest in relationships—your relationship with God first and then your relationships with others. Continually ask God for help as you walk alongside others, sometimes tripping along the way and then getting back up again, "for though the righteous fall seven times, they rise again" (Proverbs 24:16).

So, instead of going to pools of chlorine mixed with salt water, drink from "the spring of living water" (Jeremiah 2:13) and watch God work within you to eradicate loneliness and make you more like his Son.

Acknowledgments

I am so grateful for the friends in my life who have helped me understand the value of connection and community. They have helped me experience the kindness of Jesus in tangible ways that make me marvel at how good God can be by using his body of believers to nurture me whether or not I've seen the need to be nurtured.

I've already mentioned my wife, Rachael, and also Gabe Mahalík and Brian Barnett, but I'm also thinking about other deeply important people who have regularly been the hands and feet of Christ in my life: Paul Tripp, Andy Allan, John Boggs, Karl Armentrout, Rebecca Flack (who gave me an extra set of eyes on this manuscript—thank you!), Laura Materi, Ross Shearer, Denin Edwards, and the men, women, and youth in my church family at Brandywine Grace Church. To say that I'm thankful for you is a massive understatement—and not just because I'm short.

I love you all so much, and I'm extremely blessed to call you my friends.

With gratitude and affection,

Shelby

Appendix

Here are a few resources that I think will be helpful for you to check out if you want further help and instruction related to the topics we've covered in this book. Wisdom is reading widely and then applying what you've learned to everyday life. My prayer is that you take proactive steps toward wisdom by taking advantage of these resources.

Digital Identities
12 Ways Your Phone Is Changing You by Tony Reinke.

The Tech-Wise Family by Andy Crouch.

Digital Liturgies by Samuel D. James.

Porn and Casual Sex
The Death of Porn by Ray Ortlund.

Pure in Heart by Garrett Kell.

Quenched by Jessica Harris.

*5 Steps to Quit P*rn* by Ben Bennett.

resolutionmovement.org.

What's the Point? by Shelby Abbott.

Polarization (Anger)

Reactivity by Paul David Tripp.

Good and Angry by David Powlison.

The Spiritually Healthy Leader by Dave Wiedis.

Humility by Gavin Ortlund.

Anxiety and Depression

Overcoming Anxiety: Relief for Worried People by David Powlison.

A Small Book for the Anxious Heart by Ed Welch.

When the Darkness Will Not Lift by John Piper.

A Christian's Guide to Mental Illness by David Murray and Tom Karel Jr.

General Gospel Resources

Gospel Fluency by Jeff Vanderstelt.

Gospel Culture by Ray Ortlund and Sam Allberry.

New Morning Mercies by Paul David Tripp.

The Prodigal God by Tim Keller.

Essential Christianity by J.D. Greear.

Life Together by Dietrich Bonhoeffer.

Gentle and Lowly by Dane Ortlund.

Everyday Gospel by Paul David Tripp.

Endnotes

Introduction: The Loneliness Epidemic

1 D. Witters, "Loneliness in U.S. subsides from pandemic high." Gallup Survey conducted February 21–28, 2023, by Gallup as part of its Gallup Panel, a probability-based nationwide panel of 100,000 adults.

2 Kian Bakhtiari, "Gen-Z, The Loneliness Epidemic and the Unifying Power of Brands," https://www.forbes.com/sites/kianbakhtiari/2023/07/28/gen-z-the-loneliness-epidemic-and-the-unifying-power-of-brands/?sh=321de9596790 (accessed on December 11, 2023).

3 Dr. Vivek H Murthy, "Letter from the Surgeon General," https://www.hhs.gov/sites/default/files/surgeon-general-social-connection-advisory.pdf (accessed on December 11, 2023).

Chapter 3: Deepening the Disconnect: Porn and Casual Sex

4 A. De Sousa and P. Lodha, "Neurobiology of Pornography Addiction—A clinical review," *Telangana Journal of Psychiatry*, Vol 3. (2017): p. 66-70, doi:10.18231/2455-8559.2017.0016, as seen in *5 Steps to Quitting P*rn* by Ben Bennett.

5 Donald L. Hilton Jr., "Pornography addiction—a supranormal stimulus considered in the context of neuroplasticity," *Socioaffective Neuroscience & Psychology*, Vol. 3 20767 (July 19 2013), doi:10.3402/snp.v3i0.20767, as seen in *5 Steps to Quitting P*rn* by Ben Bennett.

6 M. Brand, J. Snagowski, C. Laier and S. Maderwald, "Ventral striatum activity when watching preferred pornographic pictures is correlated with symptoms of Internet pornography addiction", *Neuroimage* (April 1 2016): 129:224- 232, doi:10.1016/j.neuroimage.2016.01.033, as seen in *5 Steps to Quitting P*rn* by Ben Bennett.

7 P. Banca, L.S. Morris, S. Mitchell, N.A. Harrison, M.N. Potenza, and V. Voon, "Novelty, conditioning and attentional bias to sexual rewards," *Journal of Psychiatric Research* (January 2016): 72,91–101, doi: 10.1016/j. jpsychires.2015.10.017, as seen in *5 Steps to Quitting P*rn* by Ben Bennett.

8 Donald L. Hilton and Clark Watts, "Pornography addiction: A neuroscience perspective," *Surgical Neurology International,* Vol. 2 19 (February 21, 2011) doi:10.4103/2152-7806.76977, as seen in *5 Steps to Quitting P*rn* by Ben Bennett.

9 Ben Bennett, "5 Steps to Quit P*rn," resolutionmovement.org/wp-content/uploads/2022/07/5-Steps-to-Sexual-Wholeness.pdf, p. 5 (accessed May 9, 2024), as seen in *5 Steps to Quitting P*rn* by Ben Bennett.

10 Christina Camilleri, "Compulsive Internet Pornography Use and Mental Health: A Cross-Sectional Study in a Sample of University Students in the United States," *Frontiers in Psychology*, Vol. 11 613244 (January 12 2021), doi:10.3389/fpsyg.2020.613244.

11 "Desensitization: A Numbed Pleasure Response," *Your Brain on Porn*, https://www.yourbrainonporn.com/tools-for- change-recovery-from-porn-addiction/rebooting-basics-start-here/desensitization-a-numbed-pleasure-response/ (accessed June 6, 2022), as seen in *5 Steps to Quitting P*rn* by Ben Bennett.

12 P.J. Wright, R.S. Tokunaga, D. Herbenick, and B. Paul, "Pornography vs. Sexual Science: The Role of Pornography Use and Dependency in U.S. Teenagers' Sexual Illiteracy," *Communication Monographs* (October 12, 2021), doi:10.1080/03637751.2021.1987486, as seen in *5 Steps to Quitting P*rn* by Ben Bennett.

13 Jessica Miller and Kent S. Hoffman, D.O., https://www.addictionhelp.com/porn/statistics/ (accessed April 21, 2025).

Chapter 4: Authentic Healing: Gospel Friendships

14 A version of this anecdote by pastor J.D. Greear can be found here: https://jdgreear.com/the-primary-way-god-works-in-your-life/ (accessed September 3, 2024).

15 I first came across this reference to John Gerstner's quote in *The Prodigal God*, Tim Keller (Dutton, 2008), p. 77.

16 From the "Ministry Wives with Christine Hoover" podcast, "Friendship Between Brothers and Sisters in the Church" (an interview with Jen Wilkin and J.T. English), https://www.youtube.com/watch?v=gnxxSPWpD98 (accessed March 18, 2025).

17 "Friendship Between Brothers and Sisters in the Church."

18 "Friendship Between Brothers and Sisters in the Church."

Chapter 7: Deepening the Disconnect: Depression and Anxiety

19 The Healthy Minds Study—Student Survey, https://healthymindsnetwork.org/hms/ (accessed November 4, 2024).

20 "College Students' Anxiety, Depression Higher Than Ever, but So Are Efforts to Receive Care," https://sph.umich.edu/news/2023posts/college-students-anxiety-depression-higher-than-ever-but-so-are-efforts-to-receive-care.html#:~:text=March 9, 2023: the most significant increase since 2018 (accessed on November 4, 2024).

21 "Loneliness and Depression in Young Adults," https://www.newportinstitute.com/resources/mental-health/loneliness-and-depression-young-adults/ (accessed November 4, 2024).

22 "Loneliness and Depression in Young Adults."

23 "Loneliness and Depression in Young Adults."

Chapter 8: Authentic Healing: Gospel Involvement

24 *Forever,* Paul David Tripp (Zondervan, 2011), p. 57.

25 The genesis of this idea came from the article "The Autonomy Trap: Is Commitment Just for Suckers? A Conversion Story," James R. Wood, https://www.plough.com/en/topics/community/commitment/the-autonomy-trap (accessed November 5, 2024).

26 Source unknown, Lou Nicholes, missionary/author.

27 R.C. Sproul, "A Friend of God", https://www.ligonier.org/learn/devotionals/friend-god (accessed November 6, 2024).

Conclusion: The Long Game

28 Matthew Perry, *Friends, Lovers, and the Big Terrible Thing* (Flatiron Books, 2022), p. 7.

29 My friend Paul David Tripp says this (or something similar to this) all the time, and it's completely his original thought.

30 Something Jackie Hill Perry said while she was a guest on the *Hardly Initiated* podcast, https://www.youtube.com/live/bFXT1OmE88g (accessed November 12, 2024).

31 Another Paul Tripp-ism that I've found to be super helpful.

BIBLICAL | RELEVANT | ACCESSIBLE

At The Good Book Company we are dedicated to helping Christians and local churches grow. We believe that God's growth process always starts with hearing clearly what he has said to us through his timeless and flawless word—the Bible.

Ever since we opened our doors in 1991, we have been striving to produce resources that are biblical, relevant, and accessible. By God's grace, we have grown to become an international publisher, encouraging ordinary Christians of every age and stage and every background and denomination to live for Christ day by day and equipping churches to grow in their knowledge of God, their love for one another, and the effectiveness of their outreach.

Call one of our friendly team for a discussion of your needs or visit one of our local websites for more information on the resources and services we provide.

Your friends at The Good Book Company